To Boredom and Back

To Boredom and Back

Kent Axtell

Born-Again Marriages
P.O. Box 8
Council Bluffs, IA 51502

first printing November, 1984

artwork by Ann Donily

ISBN 0-931713-00-5

Library of Congress Catalog Number 84-091734

Dedication

To Grandpa Driver (1885-1956): His life was that of a humble, God-fearing farmer who believed in and enjoyed his family. He planted some seeds in my life as a young boy, and they grew.

To Mom and Dad: They lived and taught by example. They have always been there at each and every point in my life when I needed them, and especially now. Thanks for knowing that the job of being mom and dad lasts a lifetime.

To Lee and Carolyn Huelle: Our friends who first shared with us the key to getting our lives and marriage healed. In the face of strong resistance they persisted and were clearly the instrument without which our attempts at destroying our home would have succeeded. Thanks for not giving up on us.

To Dru and Kristin: A terrific wife and very special daughter who dared to believe in me when I wasn't worth believing in. The last ten years of walking together in a healed marriage have contained a lifetime of blessings—including another special daughter Mandy, whose name means "transformed heart." Thanks to my wife for having what it takes for us to see the dream of healing nations through healing homes while enjoying ourselves in the process. Dru, you're the greatest.

Contents

Foreword

"FOR I HATE DIVORCE," says the Lord, the God of Israel (Mal. 2:16).

"They are no more two, but one flesh. WHAT THERE-FORE GOD HAS JOINED TOGETHER, LET NO MAN SEPA-RATE!" Jesus says (Matt. 19:6, NAS).

I don't know how you interpret these scriptures, reader, but I get the distinct impression that God, the Creator of heaven and earth, the One who gives you and me our very breath and to whom we each must answer for our lives and how we've lived them, *does not have a permissive, hazy, conditional attitude toward divorce.*

I mean, when God thunders from heaven that He *hates* something, I think we ought to do our best to leave that thing alone! And when Jesus says, "I put this one-flesh unit together, and you'd better leave it that way," I believe any straight-thinking person who actually believes he's going to stand before Jesus before long ought to line up with Him on this and every other issue, and not be trying to find some way to weasel around Him. It won't work.

And yet, two out of three marriages in America today are threatened with divorce. Statistics say they don't have a chance; they're doomed. A growing high percentage of Christians, even ministers and church leaders, are swelling the statistics, giving all the same reasons non-Christians give:

> "We just grew apart; we don't have anything in common anymore."
>
> "She doesn't appreciate me. I don't think we ever knew each other."
>
> "The feelings are all gone. I love her, but I'm not *in* love with her."
>
> "The Lord wants His children to be happy, and we're not happy together. I'm happier with another person, so that must be God's will for me."
>
> "He has committed adultery, so I have scriptural grounds."
>
> "It's better for our kids for us to divorce and find other mates than for them to live in the same house with a mother and dad who fight all the time and can't get along."

Who's right and who's wrong?

Is God's expressed will out of date, irrelevant, impossible to obey in our "modern" society?

Does the church have to work out some accommodation between the stark commands of God Almighty and the complex, shifting mores of our day?

NO!

Brother, sister, you can try to rationalize if you want to, you can take your chances on convincing God He's out of touch with reality, you can try to make His Word say something it doesn't, or just ignore it and hope He'll forget about it—but I'm going with God. If I have to try to change something, Shirley and I are going to try to change *society's* (and especially the church's) attitude toward divorce rather than

God's. The Bible says that God doesn't change much, and when He announces that He *hates* divorce already, I'm not even going to try to change His thinking on that subject.

That's why we love Kent and Dru Axtell. Like Shirley and me, they just about ruined their own marriage and didn't think even God could put it back together and make it work. They were looking for a way out, and thought they'd found several.

But some meddling Christians fouled things up by praying for them and making them aware of some of the scriptures about marriage and divorce, God pitched in with a couple of miracles that resulted in their separate salvations, and before they knew it, they were back together! And not on the basis of "feelings," not because they'd "fallen" back in love, but out of mutual obedience to God and reverence for His revealed and unchanging and powerful will.

And you know what? It worked.

They found that, as terrible as their relationship had become, God could make it new. They discovered that when they prayed together for each other and their mutual problems and quit trying to have their own self-centered ways, they actually liked each other! And without really trying to, they did "fall" back in love, and today they not only have a "born-again" marriage, richer and deeper and more completely satisfying than anything they'd known before, but are able to help countless others to make the same discoveries.

God has made them "marriage doctors," and their practice is growing nationally by leaps and bounds. In many cases, they're like paramedics, called in emergency situations, where the patient appears to have died already—and they've seen many apparently terminal marriages spring back to radiant life!

Soon after Shirley and I had heard about Kent and Dru and had read some of their earliest writing, the Lord spoke to Shirley that He wanted to bruise the head of the serpent, "Divorce," here in Hollywood where media had magnified and glorified it. So we invited them to our home in Beverly Hills to conduct a week-long seminar. We invited leadership from many different churches to judge the message and take it to their churches, also many of the folks we knew who were having desperate problems with their own marriages, and some friends whose mates had already left them. Our house was filled each night for a whole week, and for most of the day on Saturday. We recorded each session so that everyone who came could have tapes of the whole seminar to feed on, to refer back to, to relive and relearn.

The meetings were so electric, and the tapes were such a clear and vibrant record of the whole seminar, that we all decided to edit them down to about fifteen hours and package them so that many thousands more could share in those meetings and the life-giving, marriage-restoring discoveries we'd all made.

Since then we've each had so many people from all over the country telling us what a miraculous difference the tapes have made in their lives and marriage relationships, and Kent and Dru's ministry has grown so rapidly, that this book was inevitable. Actually, it's long overdue, and I'm honored to add this brief foreword to it.

This book is strong medicine.

For many it will be like corrective surgery, dreaded but necessary and life-bringing. And, after all, what does the Bible say? "For the word of God is living and active and sharper than any two-edged sword, and piercing as far as the division of soul and spirit, of both joints and marrow, and able to judge the thoughts and intentions of the heart" (Heb. 4:12).

Sounds to me that God *knew* we'd need surgery and provided the perfect instrument—His Word.

And that's all Kent and Dru use: God's Word. They dig in it, they pray it, they try it, they experience it, they counsel it, they see it work, and they see people's lives and marriages transformed by it. I've never read a book more completely built on and permeated with God's Word, with as little personal interpretation thrown in.

They're not going to change God's mind or His expressed will. Instead, they've determined to share that truth with any who'll listen and work with them to see their marriages born again by God's active power and His principles in action.

Some may not agree with them, at least not all the way. Some may misunderstand and misinterpret what they say. But that's happened to almost everybody who ever tried to speak God's will and share His Word with a mixed-up, confused, and headstrong world, bent on having its own way and always looking for "loopholes" that don't exist and only lead to disaster.

Shirley and I have defended and championed many other ministers when we knew their hearts and understood what they were preaching. We know that God gives some a prophetic message, some a vision or mission, and that sometimes they or their message seem narrow or hard or "unbalanced"—but that God expects them to deliver the message in an unflinching and uncompromising way, and for the local minister to balance that message with the day-to-day situations in his congregation and the spiritual maturity or immaturity of his own hurting sheep.

What is God's message to the church? God says He *hates*

division among the brethren—that a house divided against itself cannot stand. So Satan says, "Separate them! Divide and conquer!" But read Colossians 1:17-20: Jesus holds things together; His Spirit is the Spirit of reconciliation.

Some say, "I'm divorced, but God's forgiven me." That's true. And though Jesus was a perfect sacrifice for your forgiveness, He said, "Go and sin no more!" God said obedience is better than sacrifice in 1 Samuel 15:22. And Hosea 4:6 says, "My people perish for lack of knowledge."

Well, Kent and Dru have gained knowledge we all need to examine. The truth will set us free. We can gain the knowledge to keep the destruction from happening again.

We'll all acknowledge that God tempers His will with grace; nobody measures up completely and some fall a lot further than others. Dru was married and divorced once before she even met Kent, and they both sympathize with the already divorced. But when you're trying to help people have faith for the *restoring* of a marriage, you don't provide escape clauses. You go for God's best, calling on His power rather than His forgiving grace.

As Christians read this book, *our plea* is that you heed the wise counsel of Gamaliel (Doctor of Law) as he spoke to the Jewish leaders, "If this counsel or this work be of men it will come to naught: but if it be of God you cannot overthrow it, unless you fight against God."

Jesus said to judge the tree by the fruit, and the tree of this ministry is bringing forth good fruit—healed marriages— and Jesus is getting the glory for it, because it's a work of the Holy Spirit who always glorifies Jesus.

Pray about your individual relationships with God and each other with real openness, and see if God wants to heal, redeem, or restore your marriage. He is a personal God, and He will speak to you. *This is not legalism!* This is inheritance by covenant! God's Word to His people. The taking back from Satan *all* that the blood of Jesus has already paid for—enlarging our boundaries till *all* the land God has promised us is ours.

The works of the Holy Spirit have always been controversial—"tongues," "deliverance," "healing," "faith message," "Word-confessing people"—but, *we must keep our unity and fellowship in Jesus* as we honestly investigate the messages, and we must refuse to let walls of division rise as we search. The bottom line is this: the divorce rate *must* go down in the church before we can be a witness to a lost and dying world.

Are we one in Jesus? Does the world know we're His disciples because we love one another?

"Love is very patient and kind, never jealous or envious, never boastful or proud, never haughty or selfish or rude. Love does not demand its own way. It is not irritable or touchy. It does not hold grudges and will hardly even notice when others do it wrong. It is never glad about injustice, but rejoices whenever truth wins out. If you love someone, you will be loyal to him no matter what the cost. You will always believe in him, always expect the best of him, and always stand your ground in defending him" (1 Cor. 13:4-7, Living Bible).

No! God's not through with us yet! But we're on our way.

God bless Kent and Dru Axtell. And God bless you and your marriage as you read.

PAT (and SHIRLEY) BOONE
Beverly Hills, California

1

The Family Tree. . . A Dying Species?

A trend is forming. Everywhere I am seeing people look longingly and with respect at families that are openly committed to each other. Quietly they are being drawn to admire those genuinely happy families.

Why do they catch themselves noticing so closely? It's because unless changes take place quickly, they are witnessing a rare and dying species.

It is a waning privilege for a young person to see his mom and dad living out their marriage vows, not to mention grandparents and maybe even great-grandparents who have active and happy roles in their family life.

At one point or another every couple will come to a place where some degree of compromise would seem easier than doing what is right. Husbands and wives don't evolve to a respected place in their spouse's and children's estimation merely by the accumulation of years. Rather, it is by the commitment to something far greater than an easy exit from a current difficulty. *Marriage soundness is a matter of integrity.*

I believe most people would agree there is a very real battle being fought to eliminate the strength of family ties. The obvious question for each of us is: What can *I* do to insure a healthy future to my part of the family tree?

While praying one day recently, I saw an inner vision. It was a large stack of wood in five- to six-foot lengths neatly piled beside a big stump. It was a pretty sight until God showed me what I was seeing. It was Satan's plan for the family tree—cut up and prepared for burning.

The existence of happy families is unrealistic and no more than a pipe dream if at least one partner from each marriage in the family tree is not willing to fight hard to hold their own marriage intact. So many people think their only choice in a troubled marriage is divorce. They seldom realize how much is really at stake.

Let me assure you that *there are answers that work* and that *you don't have to be a victim of negative circumstances*. Yours can be a healthy, vibrant marriage no matter what condition it is in right now.

At Born-Again Marriages we have seen hundreds of seemingly dead marriages healed because one partner chose life for that marriage. We have also seen marriages restored because concerned friends "stood in the gap" for the marriage until it was brought back together.

Society does not promote strong family ties. Marriages continue to collapse not because they can't be healed but because neither partner is fully committed to its survival. When spouses are bored with their marriage, they are susceptible to the thought that it's easier to switch partners than to do things which will cause the marriage to grow. When they choose divorce, they are simply taking what appears to be the easy way out.

Many mates don't have the courage to fight for the marriage as though a real life was at stake. A person seeing a stranger caught in a swirling river current will do anything to try to save him—even to the point of bravely risking his own life. But a person whose own marriage is threatened by a serious undertow often gives up with no struggle whatever. The evil attack is successful not due to its strength but because it met with little or no resistance.

Even the husband or wife committed to taking the marriage vows seriously will often lose hope and become indifferent when faced with repeated infidelity.

My wife, Dru, and I have people facing terrible marriage circumstances come to us for help every day. They desire to stop hurting and, of course, we also want that for them; but over and over, we have seen these people attempt to stop there and not go on to deal with the needs of the marriage itself. Some of them discover that what God's Word tells them to do about their problems is not what they wanted to hear. They fight hard for their own sanity but not for the life and health of the marriage.

One day as I interceded in prayer to find answers about how to prevent divorce, God told me that the real culprit was not adultery and all the obvious sins. It was apathy. It was not that marriages couldn't be healed but that people didn't fight hard enough to get them healed.

The great disease of apathy manifests itself in a wide variety of ways in marriages today. Apathetic marriage partners take each other so for granted that the tremendous power and fulfillment a good marriage can offer is never tapped.

Equally common is the apathetic loss of desire to fight

against one's home and family being destroyed. Too often the apathy is caused by people dwelling on intimidating circumstances rather than on God's Word which can change those temporary circumstances.

Another frequent manifestation of apathy is simple laziness. This can be seen in people knowledgeable of God's will, prayer, and spiritual warfare who gravitate to what "looks" like the better way. In a quest for God's peace, they take a counterfeit. Just for the record, the peace of God is not a vacation from spiritual responsibility as some would imagine but rather a surrendering of your time and all that you are into God's control. A "rest" then follows the diligent "doer" of God's Word which is totally foreign to the lazy, apathetic believer.

You can see another type of apathy in persons who don't know what to do in the face of horrendous marriage difficulties. They will often take on an "I-don't-care" attitude. They say, "I don't want him (or her) anymore." In their hearts the opposite is true, but since they don't know healing is actually possible for them, it becomes commonplace to hide their real feelings as a sort of self-defense.

Apathy often manifests itself as boredom. Bored people look for something exciting. They are the type who will make a change just for the sake of change. They are hoping the change will be the answer to the void they feel in their present marriage. They want more for themselves. "Looking out for Number One" is a national pastime in our culture. Commitment often is ridiculed.

The dream of what they were going to make of their marriage has left the bored people. The healthy attitude of "till death do us part" becomes conditional. The idea of spending any length of time holding a weak marriage together is, to these people, out of the question. Doing God's will is only relevant in a theoretical sense because bored persons' dissatisfaction and impatience with the problem has distracted them from their obvious mission field.

The great irony of life is that those who seek to satisfy themselves never can. Jesus taught that very thing when He said, "He that findeth his life shall lose it: and he that loseth his life for my sake shall find it" (Matt. 10:39) and "Whosoever shall exalt himself shall be abased; and he that shall humble himself shall be exalted" (Matt. 23:12).

People try to take a shortcut to happiness by pleasing only themselves. The tragic result is twofold: they don't find happiness for themselves personally, and they discover that long-range contentment in marriage eludes them as well.

Another result is that usually at least one of the spouses (not to mention the children) suffers severe trauma from the marriage failure—a trauma not found when a person follows the Holy Spirit's blueprint for the healing of that particular marriage. A person standing for a Godly outcome in his troubled marriage will discover an available inner peace *during* the circumstances that look anything but happy. He does not have to wait until after God manifests the total healing of the marriage to find the "peace of God that transcends human understanding" operating in his day-to-day life.

At the close of a Born-Again Marriages meeting, a woman approached Marilyn Conrad, the National Coordinator of "Standers International." [1]

"Could I ask you a question?" the troubled woman said. "Does the pain go away?"

Several people near the woman heard her question. Many of them had asked the same question earlier in their lives. One person quickly said, "Yes, the pain goes away. Jesus will heal your broken heart and put you back together.

"Remember, Jesus never changes and in Luke 4:18 He said, 'The Spirit of the Lord is upon me, because he hath anointed me to preach the gospel to the poor; he hath sent me *to heal the brokenhearted*, to preach deliverance to the captives, and recovering of sight to the blind, to set at liberty them that are bruised.'"

Jesus is the Master at healing broken hearts. First He works to put people like this hurting lady back together emotionally so they are then able to exercise the faith needed for God to heal their marriage. And God's healing includes every area of the marriage relationship.

The key for the survival of any marriage is to get motivation from doing what is God's pleasure instead of seeking shallow self-centered quests.

No matter what state of disintegration a marriage is in, it can be salvaged when at least *one* of the partners decides to go *God's way*. Whatever the personal, emotional, or romantic desire has or hasn't been in the marriage, a person can leave the state of marriage boredom and enter a state of marriage vibrancy and excitement he never knew existed.

Like a piece of fine furniture, marriage can have greater worth as it ages. The world says marriage starts high and tapers off from there, but God says the exact opposite—marriage starts as a baby and grows.

God's plan for marriage is that it grow "from glory to glory" right along with every other area of a Christian's life. God never intended marriage to stagnate. That is the devil's perversion of God's most treasured human relationship.

But healthy growth doesn't "just happen" when a couple puts the rings on their fingers. The Divine blueprint must be followed. It doesn't make any differance what stage the marriage is in—good, bad, indifferent, or totally deterio-rated—when a couple or even just ONE member of the couple begins acting on God's spiritual laws for marriage, that one-flesh relationship *will* begin to grow.

The marriage will be restored and then admired by all who see it when the partners put the necessary care into it. And, let me emphasize again, God needs only ONE willing partner in order to work His healing miracle for the whole marriage.

Second Corinthians 1:4 says we will be able to help others overcome the same adversities we have overcome. I have seen this time after time in Born-Again Marriages as people with formerly troubled marriages guide others into healed relationships.

Gale and Carol Conner learned firsthand God's desire to restore marriages. They were active church people. Married 23 years, they were successful and well-known in the community. But something was not right.

Love had left their marriage. Boredom had set in. They discussed the possibility of separating. After all, their three daughters were old enough to handle things on their own. Two of them were already away at college. The other was a senior in high school.

One day Carol discovered that her husband was having an affair with his secretary.

Carol didn't know what to do. Their situation was exceptionally traumatic. The speed with which things happened was a shock to everyone. They had been in the same small town for the majority of the 23 years of their marriage. Their holdings included a ranch, a potato farm, and a trucking business.

Eleven days after Carol's discovery of her husband's affair, they were divorced and the property was liquidated. They went their separate ways.

But Carol had recently asked Christ to come into her life.

Now she turned to Him for help.

Some Christian friends prayed with her, and she was baptized in the Holy Spirit. She felt bitterness, jealousy, and hatred leave. A new and different love and compassion for her husband filled her heart. She began praying for her husband's return.

Then the Holy Spirit prompted Carol to read the book of Philemon. Verse 15 of the apostle Paul's short epistle stood out: "For perhaps he therefore departed for a season, that thou shouldest receive him forever."

Carol moved to a different town to start over and hear what God wanted. God had given her a promise and a new love for Gale.

Her oldest daughter, Kathy, was a born-again Christian. She attended a Christian college and had the student body pray daily that her parents would be reunited.

Gale now had his freedom. He could live the fantasy life that seems so popular in magazines and on T.V. But he quickly discovered that the glitter was not real. The world that had looked good was so disappointing. He met other divorced men in bars, and they discussed their mutual problems.

Soon Gale's affair with his secretary deteriorated. Gale sank into depression.

Kathy talked to her father about surrendering his life to Christ.

Gale thought his daughter was just being radical. He didn't realize his former wife, his daughters, and a Christian college were praying for him.

Late one night Gale tossed in his bed. It was as if he carried a ton of weight that he couldn't shake. He was in severe depression and didn't know what to do. Out of desperation he rolled over and then knelt beside his bed. "God, if Your

Son is real, reveal Him to me," he prayed. "I need help. Come into my heart."

As he prayed, he felt the weight leave him. Then a feeling of peace overwhelmed him. He climbed in bed and quickly fell asleep.

The next morning he called his daughter and told her what he had done. Then Gale began thinking of Carol. Although they had been divorced five months, he began desiring to return to her.

One night two months later Gale flew to see Carol. They had had absolutely no communication since the divorce. One of Gale's daughters picked him up at the airport and drove him to Carol's house.

When he arrived, Carol was not home. He waited for her to return, concerned that she would have nothing to do with him. He had been unfaithful to her, and he remembered she was not the type of person to quickly "forgive and forget."

Finally, Carol returned. Gale went to the front room to meet her. When she saw him, he was surprised at the pleased look that came to her face.

"Carol, I've come home. I want to remarry you," Gale explained. "I know I've hurt you. Will you ever forgive me?"

"I forgave you seven months ago," his changed wife responded.

A short time later Gale and Carol were remarried—in the chapel of the Christian college in front of the student body that had prayed for them.

Since that time they have had the joy of helping many troubled couples discover the beauty of having a born-again marriage.

It doesn't make any difference what level of disintegration has developed in a marriage or what has been the highest level the marriage achieved in the past. It is not the natural elements in a relationship that make it great; it is the amount of Godly seed that has been planted and then given time to grow and mature.

It is not the facts and figures or the history of what went wrong in the relationship. It's not what it has or hasn't been or how far down it's gone. It is your willingness to ask God to plant His dream in you—His vision of what your one-flesh relationship's potential really is—and then allow the Master Healer to teach you how to bring this dream into reality.

In America today Satan whispers, "Divorce isn't that bad . . . You don't have to put up with this . . . You have the right to look out for yourself . . . You don't want to be hurt . . . The kids will adjust."

He attempts to destroy the family by appealing to our selfishness. A serious problem in America and in our churches is self-centeredness. "I've got to be pampered while I'm here; this is my only chance," some people say.

Jesus died for all so all those who live *might not live to or for themselves anymore but to Him* who died for them and rose again, 2 Corinthians 5:15 states.

We are in a day when the disintegration in marriages is of such a magnitude that the sheer number of divorces is a cry for help as loud as any the world has ever heard.

We must have some answers, and God has the answers!

During the last nine years that Dru and I have directed Born-Again Marriages, we have seen hundreds and hundreds of bad marriages made good and dead or broken marriages restored to life.

In that same time we have discovered answers to people's important questions about marriage healing—answers that work in the wide variety of distressing situations in which people find themselves.

[1] Standers International is an arm of Born-Again Marriages that ministers to the half of a marriage desiring healing in the face of separation, divorce, etc. These are specialized home fellowship groups that meet throughout the nation on a weekly basis. For information on starting or attending a group in your area, contact Born-Again Marriages, P.O. Box 8, Council Bluffs, IA 51502.

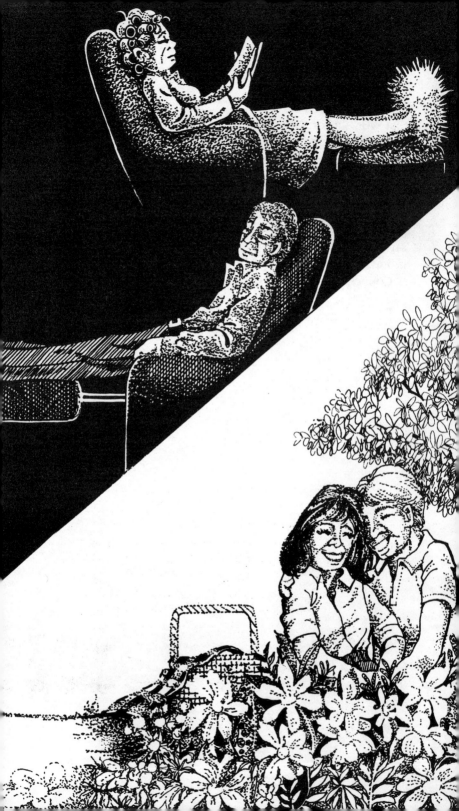

2

Is There Something A Couple Taking Each Other For Granted Can Do To Bring Healing To The Marriage?

Fifty years ago hardly any Christian would disagree with Matthew 19:6, "What God has joined together, let no man put asunder." However, in today's society, Christians are not as committed to following Christ's injunction.

This indicates that popularly accepted Christianity is changing. On the other hand, God never changes. His love is perfect and unchanging, and so are His instructions on how to live a fulfilling Christian married life.

We must align ourselves to God's standard and not try to make the Bible conform to our own or society's views. When looking at how society acts, you may think the Bible's stand is too strict. In God's eyes, however, any deviation from His Divine blueprint is compromise. He hates divorce! He hated it in Malachi's day and has not changed His mind since then simply to conform to the world's watered-down theology.

In today's society it is so easy to put personal needs and desires above considerations for others. T.V. commercials tell us to pamper ourselves and "go for the gusto"; after all, "you only go around once in life . . ." We are never shown the consequences of living only for ourselves.

The first step to strengthening a mediocre marriage is for a marriage partner to recognize his actions reflect his relationship with God.

Through the hundreds of married couples Dru and I have counseled, we've seen time after time that how a mate treats his/her partner is the same way he/she is treating God. It is a Bible axiom that how a person acts toward those he sees is how he actually treats God whom he doesn't see.

First John 4:20-21 makes a strong point: "If a man say, 'I love God,' and hateth his brother, he is a liar: for he that loveth not his brother whom he hath seen, how can he love God whom he hath not seen? And this commandment have we from him, That he who loveth God love his brother also."

We've talked to many people with troubled marriages who claim they love God very much. Yet they take their spouses for granted, not even trying to foster a growing love relationship.

Some of these people have said to me, "I'll do anything for God. When He speaks, I act. My relationship with God is strong."

But 1 John 4:20-21 contradicts them. A husband who is bored with his wife is also bored with God. And a wife who takes her husband for granted is treating God the same way.

God commands us to love our marriage partner. When we disobey His command, we are demonstrating to God very plainly just how much we care about pleasing Him. This casts a whole new light on acting in love toward that unlovable spouse. The Bible does not lie. These people are merely practicing religion rather than having a living relationship with Christ.

Each marriage partner must treat the other the way he would treat Jesus. Loyalty to marriage and to your marriage partner is not just human consideration. It is an active expression of your loyalty to God.

When I came home to Dru to reconcile our marriage, we both knew we did not love each other. However, we did love Jesus, and because of our loyalty to Him, we agreed to glean instructions from His Word as to how to treat each other.

It is very obvious in the Bible that we are to *act in love* toward one another whether we "feel" like it or not or whether the other person "deserves" it or not. We saw that God's kind of love is unconditional, and we began to DO it to the best of our abilities. If we "blew it," we sat down before God, admitted our sin to Him, and got His and each other's forgiveness and then went on.

It was one of the greatest miracles we ever experienced when, a few months later, the love between us had returned and was growing in leaps and bounds.

We had discovered the wonderful spiritual principle that when you ACT in love, the *feelings* will follow! Previously, we had missed this practical truth, and so does the rest of the world. We think we have to feel love before we act in love.

God's law of sowing and reaping is ever in effect for our benefit or detriment. When you act in love, you are sowing seeds of love, and, in time, you will reap a harvest of love. Every courting couple works this law very successfully.

Then when couples marry and allow selfishness to motivate them instead of unselfish care and love for their partners, they sow seeds of "unlove," if you will, and a crop of destruction begins to grow.

God has a purpose for everything He tells us. Everything He instructs us to do is for our happiness in this life.

It is a relief to know that when we treat our partners in love in the face of a cruel or sarcastic action towards us, we are not just being martyrs. We are wielding a powerful spiritual law to turn the very course of our marriage and home from destruction.

The second major step in the healing process is to realize that taking God or one's mate for granted is sin. It is a rejection of the precious gift He has offered.

The person must confess his sin for treating his mate and God so shabbily.

People like to make excuses for the way they act toward their mates. I've heard people say, "Well, that's just my personality" or "The way I treat my husband is simply the product of 20 years of marriage. We're not going to change."

To receive healing in marriage, we must stop rationalizing and instead call sin what it is—sin.

James 4:17 says, "To him that knoweth to do good, and doeth it not, to him it is sin."

Recognizing sin is one of the greatest leverages we have against Satan. When we confess our sins to God and repent, God is faithful to forgive us and cleanse us from all unrighteousness (1 John 1:9). Satan then no longer has power over us in that area.

Once we honestly admit that our lack of a relationship with God is the core of our problem, we can build our relationship with Him and submit to Him. Then we will start treating others the way He treats them. Our mates will see and feel the change in us because our heart's attitude will have a different complexion.

The third major step to the healing of a mediocre marriage is for the partners to realize that they are "one flesh" spiritually.

Every marriage contains three spiritual entities—the husband has his own spiritual relationship with God, the wife has hers, and their union creates the third entity known as "one flesh."

Each person individually establishes maturity in the Lord through prayer, studying the Word, and obeying God. The "one flesh" entity must establish its maturity in the same way.

A couple must pray together, share the Word together, and listen to God together; or their marriage will not have the opportunity to fully mature spiritually. It is not enough for each individual to mature in the Lord; the marriage must mature in the Lord also.

I have seen far too many marriages remain spiritually immature despite the fact that both marriage partners were growing individually in their spiritual lives. Some of the people in these marriages even had spiritual outreaches to others. However, they forgot to build the maturity of their own one-flesh relationship. The sad result was that the marriages were not satisfying and, even worse, that the marriage was blamed for the problem. That's like a couple giving birth to a healthy little baby but never feeding him anything except milk and then blaming him because he didn't grow up strong like other children.

It is far too common for a husband and a wife to be growing at a rapid rate in the Lord and for their one-flesh entity to still be a babe in diapers.

What has seemed to be rapid personal growth and maturity will become *much* deeper when the maturity of the one-flesh entity is developed with the same diligence. Praying together may seem time consuming, but it will speed up your spiritual growth.

The simple fact is that married people are under a different set of rules than single people. Any couple who truly gets the revelation that praying in the Spirit together as one flesh is the KEY to hearing from God soon will have the direction and power of God so evident in their lives that others will ask, "How do you do it?"

The greatest need this world's married spiritual leaders have is to learn to function as one flesh and develop maturity in that third entity of their relationship.

The stronger the spiritual "one-flesh" entity is, the greater will be the spiritual revelation from God in each mate's life. Greater also will be their defense against error and temptation.

Praying in the Spirit together not only enables a couple to get God's answers but keeps them acting in love toward one another in times of stress as well as in good times. Jude 20-21 says, "But ye, beloved, building up yourselves on your most holy faith, PRAYING IN THE HOLY GHOST, keep yourselves in the *love* of God . . ."

If you find yourself getting irritated easily with each other, you haven't built up your spiritual man in love by adequately praying together in the Spirit.

3

Is There Something A Couple Having Serious Problems Can Do Together To Bring About Healing?

Many couples come to Born-Again Marriages in grievous marital trouble. Some have already tried separation or are in the throes of filing for divorce. Their relationship is devastated.

If a couple is at all willing to save their marriage and work to discover how a good marriage can be developed, God will help them do it. God is *for* marriage.

Good marriages don't just happen. I never have met anyone with a happy marriage who didn't have some knowledge of why that happiness and satisfaction existed in their marriage.

God does not arbitrarily give some people good marriages and others bad marriages. There are practical, identifiable principles that work in these marriages as predictably as the law of gravity works. God reveals the steps, and those who develop good marriages by using them become able to help others.

Throughout the nation, couples with Born-Again Marriages who have had the worst problems are becoming the most effective in helping others. With joy they are able to help others with, as 2 Corinthians 1:4 says, the help wherewith they themselves were helped of God.

Let me put to rest the idea that some can make it and some just can't. God wants to heal every marriage, and God knows how to heal *every* marriage. The question God needs to hear from those with problems is not, "Should we get a divorce?" but, "How do we get healed?" That is the point at which God smiles and says, "Now we're getting somewhere."

The very first thing a couple in serious marital trouble must do is avoid strife.

James 3:16 says, "Where envying and strife is, there is confusion and every evil work."

Couples experiencing strife also experience confusion. Once strife happens, they are more prone to wrong decisions and an inability to defend themselves from the devil than at any other time. Yielding to strife is like standing up in the middle of a war, waving your hat at the enemy, and saying, "Hey—aim your guns over here!"

One of the most common manifestations of this confusion is that each one thinks the other person is the problem. I have talked with many couples whose marriages are devastated. Almost always each partner blames the other.

That attitude, when left to fester, strips the marriage of its strength and aims it toward certain destruction.

On the other hand, consider where the attitude portrayed in Matthew 7:5 would send a couple: "First cast out the beam out of thine own eye; and then shalt thou see clearly to cast out the mote out of thy brother's eye."

This boldly says *how you* can set the stage to help your partner. It is not that God is ignoring your partner's faults. He knows more of them than you ever will. It's just that God is always available with answers rather than being blinded by the problems.

We have seen repeatedly that it is not your circumstances that are going to change first—it's you!

Instead of criticizing, pray for your partner and bind the devil from continuing to influence him/her in his/her obvious sins or shortcomings. Then ask God what areas He wants *you* to work on.

One wife whose husband was in blatant adultery humbled herself to God in this manner. She was shocked and amazed as God revealed to her, in many ways, how she had hurt her husband. Previously, all she could see was his "big" sin of adultery. She had not recognized her "small" sins that could have driven him to find understanding and praise elsewhere. By this wife's willingness to please Jesus, He now had free rein to bring love back into this home.

The direction in which you are looking determines how you feel. In any set of circumstances, if you face toward the impossible appearance of things, you will begin feeling the same as the problem—discouraged, frustrated, hopeless, in despair. On the other hand, from that same exact point of circumstances, if you turn and face toward the answer, you will begin feeling the same as the answer—encouraged, hopeful, determined, strengthened. The light at the end of the tunnel is a tremendous motivator.

The devil has a destructive counterfeit to that light. He says the light can be found by divorce and a change of partners. He's a liar.

Troubled couples who remain in strife stay confused, not

really knowing who or what the real enemy is. Often they make matters worse by carelessly and critically talking about each other and to each other.

Galatians 5:14-15 says, "For the whole Law [concerning human relationships] is complied with in the one precept, You shall love your neighbor as yourself. But if you bite and devour one another [in partisan strife], be careful that you [and your whole fellowship] are not consumed by one another" (Amp.).

Proverbs 17:14 states, "The beginning of strife is as when water first trickles [from a crack in a dam]; therefore stop contention before it becomes worse and quarreling breaks out" (Amp.).

Contention is one of the warning signs that strife is about to occur. A couple experiencing an undercurrent of friction or irritation should be very wary of entering into strife. If they deal with the problem early, they will avoid having the dam of harmful words and actions break.

Proverbs 13:10 says, "Only by pride cometh contention." The truth of that verse is far-reaching.

It is pride that makes us want to respond with sarcasm, self-defense, or a cutting jab to hurt our partner in return for a thoughtless remark or completely unjust accusation they may have made toward us.

It is a true mark of spiritual maturity and our fidelity to Jesus when we discipline our natural desire and refuse to yield to pride which would bring about contention.

If you have trouble in this area, confess God's answer every day from 1 Peter 2:19-23 out loud, and God will cause His Word to become a part of your personality:

For this is thankworthy, if a man *for conscience toward God* (Here again it boils down to, "Do I want to please

God or myself?") endure grief, suffering wrongfully. For what glory is it, if, when ye be buffeted for your faults, ye shall take it patiently? but if, when ye do well, and suffer for it, ye take it patiently, *this is acceptable with God*. For even hereunto were ye called: because Christ also suffered for us, leaving us an example, that ye should follow his steps: Who did no sin, neither was guile found in his mouth: Who, when he was reviled, reviled not again; when he suffered, he threatened not; but committed himself to him that judgeth righteously.

Here is where the "nitty-gritty" of the Christian life either works or doesn't: at home between husband and wife—the most intense relationship that exists on the earth.

Jesus is so in love with the home and family and the bond He created between man and wife that He knows the suffering that occurs with hurtful words. So in His marriage Rule Book, He's provided our solution. You abide by 1 Peter 2:19-23, and go into your bedroom or bathroom and say, "Jesus, You know I didn't deserve that cutting remark, but I forgive my mate and ask You to vindicate me. You reveal to my partner that those words were unjust. I give You the hurt I feel. Thank You, Jesus."

From personal experience, Dru and I can tell you that you will almost feel Jesus patting you on the back and saying, "Well done. I'm so proud of you."

In time, your partner will say, "Honey, I don't know what came over me. I'm so sorry I said that." And the devil . . . well, he lost another opportunity to assist your marriage in deteriorating any further.

Being a Christian is not carrying six Bibles and yelling, "Praise the Lord," in church every Sunday for a few hours. It is living God's principles at home where no one—except

Jesus—sees how you treat your partner.

Remember, it takes two to be in strife and only *one* to keep strife from happening. This point applies both to couples working together as well as in situations where only one is actively working to develop a Godly marriage.

When the marriage is no longer a victim of strife, the confusion will end. The couple will start gaining perspective. Their decisions are no longer emotional reactions.

What you must realize is that the real enemy is Satan who wants to destroy marriage. Confusion, which is the direct by-product of strife, is a necessary step in the destruction process. Start battling him instead of each other. And start winning!

A second major requirement in healing a bad marriage is to use words constructively.

Verbal abuse can be just as damaging in a marriage as physical abuse. Many people who are "too civilized" to strike each other with their fists use words to destroy their marriage partners. In fact, the mental anguish suffered from a constant barrage of hateful words can finally result in physical problems.

Words are containers with which we carry spiritual substance from place to place. We can carry negative substance and "dump it" on someone, or we can carry positive substance to give others life.

The Word of God gives very high priority to words. Proverbs 4:23-24 admonishes, "Keep thy heart with all diligence; for out of it are the issues of life. Put away from thee a froward mouth, and perverse lips put far from thee."

And James 3:2-5 describes the power of the tongue:

> If any man offend not in word, the same is a perfect man, and able also to bridle the whole body. Behold, we put

bits in the horses' mouths, that they may obey us; and we turn about their whole body. Behold also the ships, which though they be so great, and are driven of fierce winds, yet are they turned about with a very small helm, whithersoever the governor listeth. Even so the tongue is a little member, and boasteth great things. Behold, how great a matter a little fire kindleth!

Words reveal the problems of the person using them just as much as they affect the person hearing them. Matthew 12:34 says, "For out of the abundance of the heart, the mouth speaketh."

If a person is able to control his words, he will be able to control the rest of his life. This means a person can get his marriage back in order if he will control what he says.

Words also dictate the destiny of the speaker. Matthew 12:37 says, "For by thy words thou shalt be justified, and by thy words thou shalt be condemned." Spouses who try to strike back at their marriage partners through words are actually condemning themselves.

When prospective marriage partners court each other, their blossoming relationship is built with words. Usually the courting starts with the man asking the woman for a date. The couple "sizes each other up" largely through conversations. As the dating experience continues, they express their feelings through terms of endearment. Finally, the man asks the woman to marry him.

When Dru and I courted each other, neither of us wanted to get serious. This gave us ample opportunities for pleasant conversations and a relaxed dating atmosphere. The more we talked and experienced things together, the more we enjoyed each other's presence.

At the time, I was a salesman. I made my money largely

through an ability to converse with people. From the very beginning of our relationship, I noticed that her approval and encouragement fueled my abilities. She told me how good I was and admired all my accomplishments. It was fun to report winning a sales contract to her. She even made small things seem important.

When Dru and I married, we took a six-month honeymoon. I resigned all training and management responsibilities and worked only enough to earn our necessary cash. Because of her influence, I was soon earning as much in two days as I had in a full week before. Dru believed in me and said so. I responded by being more productive than I realized I could be.

After the honeymoon, I gradually settled back into the full-time work routine. I had a number of salesmen under me, and to keep them highly motivated for success took an extremely high percentage of my time. Consequently, Dru was forced into finding activities and interests of her own. For a time she continued being supportive of me. But as I lived more and more for money and the future, I grew too busy to share the small, intimate things she enjoyed.

My higher-than-average financial success didn't seem to do anything for her anymore.

A few years into our marriage, our relationship changed, and Dru and I were no longer as encouraging to each other. My abilities and self-image changed proportionally.

I began trying to fill the void in my life by doing things that were totally contrary to the marriage vows. This, of course, made things worse. As the void widened, my abilities dropped even more. In one frustrating year my income plummeted $35,000.

I probably looked much the same to those around me, but I didn't feel the same. Even though I still drove fancy cars and dressed for success, things were not the same inside. I felt like a shell of the man I had been. Self-gratification was a poor second to a happy marriage.

Our marriage began with good words. It collapsed largely because of bad words. When the Bible says that the power of life and death is in the tongue, it is not kidding. I asked God one day why such a high emphasis on words was placed in the Bible. He reminded me that more important than comfortable homes, fine cars, office complexes, and airplanes are people—that all the "things" are only important because people need them.

He then showed me the reason words are so important: with words we build each other up; with words we tear each other down.

By the time Dru accepted Christ into her life, our marriage was virtually non-existent. We no longer loved each other, our divorce was filed, I had moved out and had plans to marry someone else. We were also on the verge of bankruptcy.

Dru did not want the divorce. She knew it would deeply harm our daughter. And she still remembered the happiness of our early years together. She believed God could restore that kind of marriage and began praying for me. Through a number of miracles, I too became born again.

After a time, the Lord told me to go back to Dru. That wasn't at all what my emotions wanted, but I desired to obey God. I knew I desperately needed His wisdom in my life.

Our mutual decision was to yield ourselves whole-heartedly to God. As our love for Him grew, our love for each other came back to life as well. During this time we were very careful what we said to each other. Our words once again played an important part in our marriage. This time they were words of life, and despite some trying circumstances, speaking the words of Jesus brought healing.

What comes out of a person is what has been placed there previously. Sometimes in the pressures of day-to-day living we may do some irrational things we quickly regret. It may be a flippant remark or a "dig" against our mate. It may be worse.

Shortly after Dru and I were reconciled, we had a misunderstanding as we sat at the kitchen table. Before I knew what was happening, a coffee cup filled with hot coffee came flying at me from Dru's direction.

I was not harmed, but Dru was. She couldn't believe what she had just done. Loss of temper was not a part of her personality even before she was born again. She left the room quickly and went into the bathroom. There she began praying, asking God what had come over her.

Very quickly the Lord revealed that she had picked up a spirit of temper and must rebuke it. Using the name of Jesus, she told that spirit it had no power over her and that it had to go. She asked God's forgiveness and then came back and apologized to me. She never gave the spirit of temper access to her life again.

This incident taught us an important lesson. The devil did not bow out gracefully when I came home to restore our marriage. He aimed both barrels at us. We did not learn to operate in God's principles overnight. Being new Christians, we did not always recognize the devil's tactics. Little by little, during stressful situations, Dru had allowed the tendency toward temper to gain access into her life. Dru and I quickly learned that we must both guard our hearts with all diligence, for out of it are the issues of life, as Proverbs 4:23 says.

Our hearts are designed to be generators of God's power.

He wants the freedom to do things through us. When we guard what goes into our hearts, we will act correctly in pressure situations.

If, however, we adopt the world's actions and thought patterns, we will act worldly under pressure.

As God healed our marriage, Dru and I learned another rule that every couple with serious marriage problems should practice: *Go to Jesus for answers; don't expect them mentally*.

Shortly after I came back home to Dru, we made an agreement that either of us could call a prayer time anytime we needed it. In advance we agreed to pray together if any of the old or new frictions, disappointments, embarrassments, or hurt feelings should occur. We determined not to sort out all the problems mentally. Instead, we would take what we saw as a problem and give it to Jesus in prayer together.

Dru and I both have strong opinions. We had to go to God many times in what we called our "white-knuckle prayer sessions." We knelt together and held hands, often with much turmoil inside and between each other.

Each of us took our grievances to God instead of to each other. "Father, in Jesus' name, we come before You," Dru prayed. "There's something that Kent does that disturbs me." Then she identified the problem, and we sought the Lord's solution. At other times I was the one praying, identifying something Dru did that bothered me.

We were not trying to put the other one in guilt. We didn't try to blame each other as the cause of every problem. We were beyond the point of caring about who was right. We weren't interested in getting our own ways. Instead, we wanted God's way.

We had tried our own ways before and had failed miserably. I can't tell you how good it felt to use principles that actually worked, bringing peace and contentment to those tense situations.

Our prayer sessions were so fruitful that our reverence for God grew enormously. And we saw that He required our obedience. We had to have Him and His wisdom for our marriage to work, and He also had to have our willingness to cooperate.

We had struggled so hard in times past to get things to work out but with no success. Counselor after counselor had recommended divorce. With all that behind us, we were really impressed with the results of our "white-knuckle prayer sessions."

Within a few hours or, at most, a few days, depending on the extent of the problem, we had a solution. There was not one time that God failed to give us the answer that brought harmony between us.

What is the key? Being honest before Him. In essence we practiced what Colossians 3:13-15 directs:

Be gentle and forbearing with one another and, if one has a difference (a grievance or complaint) against another, readily pardoning each other; even as the Lord has freely forgiven you, so must you also [forgive]. And above all these [put on] love and enfold yourselves with the bond of perfectness—which binds everything together in ideal harmony. And let the peace (soul harmony which comes) from the Christ rule *(act as umpire continually)* in your hearts—deciding and settling with finality all questions that arise in your minds—[in that peaceful state] to which [as members of Christ's] one body you were also called [to live] (Amp.).

When we let Christ be the umpire, we discovered that

not only could we handle problems, but our decisions were being made with greater ease as well.

It's amazing what big mistakes people make who think they can do things without using God's system. Sooner or later, doing it "my way" doesn't pan out.

We also had to walk in another major spiritual principle: *Forgive at every opportunity.*

Many people have been hurt more severely by unforgiveness which has been allowed to accumulate within themselves than by the actual acts committed against them by someone else. They stew in their own bitterness, claiming they were right and others were wrong.

Dru and I discovered that only as we extended forgiveness to others did we receive forgiveness ourselves. We began practicing the directions in Mark 11:25-26: "And when ye stand praying, forgive, if ye have ought against any: that your Father also which is in heaven may forgive you your trespasses. But if ye do not forgive, neither will your Father which is in heaven forgive your trespasses."

We had to learn to forgive at every opportunity. We were not to count the times we forgave. We were to *live* in forgiveness.

We couldn't have forgiveness unless we gave it away. We couldn't receive forgiveness from God unless we were willing to extend forgiveness to each other and to anyone else whom we felt ever hurt or wronged us.

I began seeing that all of God's principles work the same. As I forgave, I was forgiven. As I loved others, I received love. As I gave to God, He blessed me back.

When I forgave Dru for a remark or something she did, I felt clean. I became healed as I forgave.

One day I dropped Dru off at a ladies' afternoon Bible study while I ran some errands. When I came back, she hopped in the car and said, "I gave away our television set."

With no warning, I found myself having to avoid strife and act in forgiveness at the same time.

I asked which television she had given away, and, sure enough, it was the Magnavox with the nice remote controls. To keep from saying something wrong, I said nothing.

An evangelist and his family had just moved to town and had sold all their furniture to make the move. At the ladies' Bible study his wife made a prayer request for a television. Dru had quickly responded, "You've got it."

The fact is, we probably would have given it to them. However, we had not discussed it and prayed about it together. Not making sure we agreed was a violation of one of the basics we were still learning to live by.

By the time we were half way home, I managed to discuss the weather just to in some way break the silence until I could be alone to pray and have a talk with myself and God.

When we got home, I went down to my office and prayed in the Spirit. In only a minute or two I knew what to do. First, I told God that I agreed with Dru's decision, and then I told the devil he wasn't going to use this in any way to cause friction or strife.

Next, I told God that I forgave Dru for making a decision before we were in agreement. I also promised Him that I would never bring it up to her.

Then I went upstairs and said, "Let's pray over this gift and take it to them." I'm not sure, but I think I heard a long sigh of relief just then from Dru. We prayed, loaded up the television, and delivered it to our new friends. As we brought it in, the husband exclaimed, "Wow . . . that's a good one."

I felt like saying, "Of course! My wife doesn't give away junk." Instead, I just smiled and enjoyed the opportunity to be a blessing, resist the devil, and please God all at the same time.

On the way home I felt God's smile on us as never before. We had victory in a situation that required constructive use of our words, a promptness to forgive, and a rejection of strife. And, by the way, a few months later I won a much nicer television set from my company in a sales contest.

4

Is There Something A Husband Or Wife Can Do Alone When Their Partner Wants Marriage Healing But That Partner Can't Seem To Do The Things That Will Bring The Healing?

I have met many people who have partners with major problems—alcoholism, gambling, compulsive spending, or habitual adultery. These people desperately want to be rid of their compulsions and have good marriages, but they don't know how.

We've found the most significant key is in teaching their mates how to do spiritual battle for them. The one-flesh partner is in the most powerful position spiritually to rescue his troubled mate once he acquires the knowledge from God's Word.

I sympathize with people who are addicted to destructive habits. I was once addicted.

When I was single, I was never impressed with people who were untrue to their mates. The idea of a girlfriend or a mistress on the side was not "cool" in my book. I was confident that when I married, I would always be true to my wife.

Dru and I were married only about four months when, one day, while I was driving alone through a residential neighborhood, I had a vivid thought of committing adultery flash through my brain. Dru and I weren't unhappy, we hadn't just had a fight, there wasn't someone enticing me—there was no explanation for this unexpected inner motivation.

I was embarrassed and even repulsed by the thought I had just had. Yet, there it was all the same.

I rejected the idea and went on my way, but a few days later the same tormenting thought intruded my mind. It made me feel like I was two people—one who was a good, honest, and loyal husband and another who was exactly what I disapproved of in some other men for whom I had no respect.

As time passed, I continued to struggle with thoughts of adultery. Finally, temptation was turned into reality. James 1:15 explains it well, "When lust hath conceived, it bringeth forth sin . . ."

Words cannot describe the disgust I felt for myself. After I had yielded to the act of adultery, I was so ashamed. I said to myself, "*I will never do that again!*"

I was only 21 years old and had already been unfaithful to my wife. As a salesman I was accustomed to setting a goal and achieving it. I would frequently determine a thing and see it come to pass. The year before, I had desired a substantial income and had achieved it. I had wanted a new, red Oldsmobile convertible and was now driving it.

I was confident that in my marriage I could set a goal also and achieve it. I determined never again to be untrue to Dru. I had fallen once but would never let it happen again.

The next six years of my life could easily be several different books. First of all, my life was like a sordid novel because my immorality became disgustingly rampant.

Certainly my life was an enigma to me because in the midst of all the junk in which I was involved, I myself couldn't explain why I was doing it. I was hooked on sin. Those around me may have thought I was having the time of my life—a girl in every port. But within me was an agonizing and frustrating search for freedom to once again be a man I could respect.

My life became a tragedy because Satan had come to steal, kill, and destroy. I suffered great loss, agony, and pain. I was hurt and so was my family—just as countless others are who are caught in the web of adultery.

All the while God waited with His Divine epistle for my life until I was at the end of my rope. He orchestrated intercessors to cross my path and pray for me. He placed a couple in Dru's life to lead her to Jesus and encourage her faith for me to be born again and to return to her.

By the time I had left home and filed for divorce at the end of those eleven sad but true years, I was hopelessly ensnared by the addiction to adultery. I had lost not only the ability but even the desire to resist that evil spirit. I was demon possessed. On my own I could never have recovered.

Proverbs 6:32 says that when a man commits adultery with a woman, he destroys his own soul. I still wanted my marriage to work; yet adultery was clearly and openly my lifestyle. I was out of control.

The question now is, What can a person do who is married to someone caught in a sin trap such as I was?

Christian mates with partners who can't or don't want to free themselves from their sinful habits can do several things to promote deliverance.

One of the most important things spouses can do to help their mates is to believe in them.

There is tremendous power for change and a sense of security when a person feels someone believes in him.

When I was a small child, there was an incident involving Grandpa Driver, my mother's father, that made a lasting impression on me. One day while some of my cousins and I were playing at my grandparents' house, we broke a window in the porch. Although it was an accident, I was sure we were in big trouble. Grandpa came outside and looked at the broken window. One of the adults began to apologize for our actions. "Oh, I'd rather have the children here. We can replace the window," Grandpa said gently.

What I discovered from that situation was that even we kids were important. His act of compassion and love made a lifelong impression on this four-year-old boy. People need to belong; they need the love and compassion of others. Mates—especially those in addictions—need help believing in themselves.

A person trapped in a habit has a terrible time believing in himself. He may be proficient in twenty other areas of his life, but one bad habit can negate all the confidence in the other areas.

People enslaved by addiction find themselves continually on the edge of discouragement.

This type of discouragement is subtle and a little different from discouragement as it is normally understood. It isn't sad-faced despair. Rather it is the inability to see themselves being normal in a certain area. They vow to change (as I often did when I was addicted to adultery) but fail repeatedly. This leaves them unable to believe in themselves. The discouragement eventually causes them to stop even trying to change.

For example, suppose a woman is married to a good, honest man. At one vulnerable moment a man makes a pass at her and she falls. Not wanting to live in immorality, she chooses not to repeat what she has done—but at another time, in another place she falls again. The discouragement I'm speaking of can be saying to her, "You aren't able to make it as a married woman. You need to be single so doing this type of thing won't be anyone's business but your own." She may actually believe this whispered lie of the enemy.

The discouragement is perhaps even worse for a person who is an alcoholic. The person may mean it from the bottom of his heart when he says he's going to quit drinking, but when he repeatedly can't keep his word even to himself, he is on the verge of despair. Without someone who says, "I believe in you," he could easily slip into that "live like hell" attitude of "I can't do anything about it anyway."

Discouraged people make decisions based on negative circumstances rather than directing their lives through wise choices. They continue to sink lower and fail more. Often they say, "I'm just going to live in sin" or "I can't resist this thing, so why not join it?"

Then, instead of sneaking their compulsion, they sacrifice their mate and family and flaunt their sinful habit. They are discouraged and have no hope.

Deep inside, they want to stop. They want someone to help them, but either they don't know how or pride keeps them from expressing their need. We have all heard of criminals who committed crimes in such a way that they were sure to be caught. They wanted someone to help them stop.

We've all seen children do many things, often very negative, to get their parents' attention. They throw temper tantrums when they're young and wild parties when they're older. They want someone to love them enough to discipline them. They want help. They need parents to believe in them enough to show them right from wrong.

A discouraged mate desperately needs someone to believe in him. Their partner must be the one to anchor the troubled person to righteousness.

Romans 15:1 says, "We then that are strong ought to bear the infirmities of the weak, and not to please ourselves." If we have any strength, we must help those who are weaker.

To help others, we should also practice the admonition in Philippians 4:8: "Whatsoever things are true, whatsoever things are honest, whatsoever things are just, whatsoever things are pure, whatsoever things are lovely, whatsoever things are of good report; if there be any virtue, and if there be any praise, think on these things." The Amplified Bible says to "fix your minds on them."

If we don't fix our minds on the positive things, we are disobeying God's Word. We are sinning. Too often people dwell on each other's problems—talking about them, even accusing their mates or belittling them in front of friends. Those who dwell on the weaknesses in others are in sin themselves.

Lynne Wilford, who heads our counseling staff at Born-Again Marriages, counseled a woman whose husband was living in deep sin. He had hurt the woman deeply, and now she was looking for someone to help her justify leaving the marriage.

For a time Lynne listened to the woman and was a friend to her. Then she showed the woman scripturally that God hates divorce. She told her, "You can pray, and your husband will change. God will heal your marriage."

"That can't be what you think," the troubled woman said. "You, of all people, know how terrible he has been to me."

"If you want to know what *I* think, I think you should

divorce him," Lynne replied. "He's a real jerk. Now, do you want to know what I think, or do you want to know what God thinks?"

Lynne's words shocked the lady into reality. Her marriage would not have been healed had she continued in her own self-pity.

People's opinions are not as important as God's Word, and those who dwell on problems usually formulate negative ones. Many times they read the Bible only to confirm what they have already made up their minds to believe. They go to counselors to get help justifying their actions.

Americans "write others off" pretty easily. In our culture it is more common to give up on relationships than to work through the problems and get healing. People's opinions usually seek the lowest level of truth. God's Word, on the other hand, is the highest level of truth.

Believing opinions causes people to become doubters. A person who meditates on God's Word and in its high level of truth will be anointed to believe the best of his spouse. He will gain the spiritual knowledge and the substance of faith needed to "see" his partner healed and whole and living for Jesus. As the person is built up in his "most holy faith," he will be able to help that spouse become whole.

First Corinthians 13:7-8 says, "Love bears up under anything and everything that comes, is ever ready to believe the best of every person, its hopes are fadeless under all circumstances and it endures everything [without weakening]. Love never fails" (Amp.).

Verse 13 completes the thought, "And so faith, hope,love abide . . . love, true affection for God and man, growing out of God's love for and in us . . . these three, but the greatest of these is love" (Amp.).

As a spouse opens up to God and sees his mate through

God's eyes, he can let God's love in him flow to his spouse. The partner with the problems will recognize that someone believes in him. He then can dare to take the first steps toward change.

I am not suggesting that in this act of believing in the person, you are walking in ignorance of the circumstances. I'm not saying that if you ignore the problem, it will go away. If you ignore the problem, it will grow!

What we are to do is lay the foundation for keeping the person as on track as possible while we *pray* the miracle-power of God into his life. We are being a lifeline to him while we *use the name of Jesus to break the powers of hell* that have come against that loved one.

According to Ephesians 6:12, "We wrestle not against flesh and blood." Although it may seem you are fighting against your partner, in reality, you are fighting *for* him and against the devil.

When you catch the revelation of this truth, you'll never again be vulnerable to hurtful words and actions from your partner. Since the devil is a liar, you'll not believe the lies; you'll go to your prayer closet and in the name of Jesus thwart all the devil's tactics.

With this valuable knowledge of God tucked in your heart, you'll be able to enter the spiritual battle *knowing* God and you will win.

You might say, "If I try to help, I'll just be pulled down with my partner."

Well, make no mistake about it; in your own strength you will probably fail. You and God must do it together. The key to success is in keeping yourself strengthened personally in the Word of God and in prayer.

I have had the honor of observing those beautiful soldiers of the Cross whose circumstances were horribly painful.

Yet they have become healed, whole, strong Christians right in the midst of battle. God is able to be such a present help in times of trouble that they are no longer merely "hanging on." With God's Word becoming first place in their lives, they find themselves tenaciously using their faith to defeat the devil's ploys time and again. They become stabilizers in situations otherwise doomed to misery and defeat.

These are men and women about whom the world would say, "Life is passing them by." But they have counted the cost and, like Paul in Philippians 4:13, say, "I can do all things through Christ which strengtheneth me."

A caring spouse should deliberately fast for his marriage partner.

Fasting is one of the most powerful weapons God has given the believer for the tearing down of Satan's strongholds. Just look at the results of fasting listed in Isaiah 58:6-7: "Is not this the fast that I have chosen: to loose the bands of wickedness, to undo the heavy burdens, and to let the oppressed go free, and that ye break every yoke? Is it not to deal thy bread to the hungry, and that thou bring the poor that are cast out to thy house? when thou seest the naked, that thou cover him; and that thou hide not thyself from thine own flesh?"

A careful reading of verses eight through twelve will quicken many promises to the person willing to apply God's fast:

> Then shall thy light break forth as the morning, and thine health shall spring forth speedily: and thy righteousness shall go before thee; the glory of the Lord shall be thy rereward. Then shalt thou call, and the Lord shall answer; thou shalt cry, and he shall say, Here I am. If thou take

away from the midst of thee the yoke, the putting forth of the finger, and speaking vanity; and if thou draw out thy soul to the hungry, and satisfy the afflicted soul; then shall thy light rise in obscurity, and thy darkness be as the noon day. And the Lord shall guide thee continually, and satisfy thy soul in drought, and make fat thy bones: and thou shalt be like a watered garden and like a spring of water, whose waters fail not. And they that shall be of thee shall build the old waste places: *thou shalt be called, The repairer of the breach, The restorer of paths to dwell in*.

Using your spiritual weapon of fasting allows God to work on your behalf to loose those bands of wickedness and oppression and break the yokes that the devil has used to enslave your partner. God says you'll be healthy, He'll guide you continually, and YOU shall be called the repairer of the breach, the restorer of paths to dwell in!

The deeper we delve into God's Word, the more we see that God has not left us to face the devil's onslaught against marriage and family by ourselves. He's given us many weapons which "are not carnal, but mighty through God to the pulling down of strongholds" (2 Cor. 10:4).

At Born-Again Marriages we have an organization known as the "Repairers and Restorers." Members meet in groups of eight and take turns fasting and praying for each other's needs. Each of the eight fasting days is manned by an individual, a couple, or a family. Each member discovers the blessing of having others willing to pray and fast for him and his family and the honor of fasting and praying for others of "like precious faith." (For more information, you may write to Born-Again Marriages, P.O. Box 8, Council Bluffs, Iowa 51502.)

Another thing spouses must do to help their mates is to speak the Word about them.

This is a very simple process of taking Scriptures that show God's will and then speaking that actual passage with the loved one's name in it. It sounds simple and is definitely one of the easier things to do. But is it ever powerful.

A wife could pray Ephesians 5:25 over her husband as follows: "Father, in Jesus' name I pray that my husband, John, will love me like Jesus loved the Church and that he will give of himself for me."

A husband might pray Proverbs 31:12 over his wife: "Father, in Jesus' name I pray that my wife will do me good and not evil all the days of her life."

Some other good verses are Galatians 5:16, John 8:12, Ephesians 4:32, and Philippians 1:6.

God says in Isaiah 55:11, "So shall my word be that goeth forth out of my mouth: it shall not return unto me void, but it shall accomplish that which I please, and it shall prosper in the thing whereto I sent it."

It's no wonder that the Word, when spoken by a Christian, makes such a difference in the lives of loved ones.

The area that requires discipline here is to speak *God's* Word about a mate instead of our own words. A common tendency is to complain and perhaps look for some sympathy from friends, parents, or prayer partners.

Most Christians do not realize the spiritual authority of their words. With our words we have the power to decree things, according to Job 22:28: "You shall also decide and decree a thing and it shall be established for you, and the light [of God's favor] shall shine upon your ways" (Amp.).

We can either *decree* our partner healed, delivered, and home; or we can *decree* that "their drinking is getting heav-

ier" or "he says he doesn't love me anymore" or "the adulterous affair is winning."

Whatever the sin may be, you, the one-flesh partner, have
a choice. God's Word says two witnesses establish any matter. So, by your words, you can agree with what God says
and allow Him to "hasten to perform His word." Or you can
agree with the negative-looking circumstances and say they
are getting worse and worse—thus giving the devil authority to continue his evil work.

What you must guard against is speaking the Word and
decreeing your marriage healed and then speaking the
opposite in an off-guard moment (when a friend calls and
asks how your mate is treating you these days) by telling
them all the rotten-looking circumstances.

You must not lie about your circumstances. Instead, program yourself to say what God says about it. You agree with
and decree God's will for your marriage rather than the
devil's.

When a person starts declaring God's Word concerning
his mate's problem, then supernatural changes begin. Not
only does the person speaking increase his own spiritual
vision, but he gives God and His angels legal right to enforce
the transforming power of the Word in his partner's heart.

Hebrews 1:14 talks about angels and their assignment
from God to help the individual believers. It says, "Are they
not all ministering spirits, sent forth to minister for them
who shall be heirs of salvation?"

Psalm 103:20 says, "Bless the Lord, ye his angels, that
excel in strength, that do his commandments, hearkening
unto the voice of *his* word."

The Word of God when spoken by a single-minded Christian becomes an instruction for those heavenly messengers!
What power to have those mighty angels following our

loved ones everywhere, whispering God's words to them. In the name of Jesus, dispatch your partner's angels to go right to the bars or to the adulterous meetings with him!

Hosea 2:6-7 says God hedged up Hosea's adulterous wife's way with thorns so she could not find her lovers. God will do the same for your partner in adultery when you speak His Word. He will send His angels forth on your behalf.

When Lee and Carolyn Huelle began to pray for our salvation, Dru was dancing in a bar one night with a fellow. A voice inside her clearly said, "You don't belong in a place like this."

Dru didn't know where the voice came from although she agreed with it and in her heart said, "But I don't know where else to go."

We now know her angel was working, and God soon gave her the rest of the answer because of Lee and Carolyn's intercessory prayer.

One of my favorite examples of the fruit of confessing God's Word is what happened to Mike and Marilyn Phillips.

They were in the process of becoming a typical divorce statistic, only with a little more flair than most. (That means they were expending more energy in the process than others do.)

Michael was a businessman who had found ways of making lots of money. He developed an attitude of doing what he wanted when he wanted, and it didn't matter much to him what his wife thought about it.

Marilyn came to the point where Michael's drinking and running around were more than she could stand. She told God, "I'm going to divorce him."

God spoke right back to her and said, "No, you're not."

For a time that gave her the courage to hang on, but it

wasn't for long. Michael's activity became more and more humiliating to the point that she absolutely could not tolerate it any longer. She said, "God, I don't care. I'm going to divorce him."

God replied, "No, you're not."

"Well, if I'm not going to divorce him, how are we going to get it healed?" (This is the kind of situation I mentioned before where God smiles and says, "Now we're getting somewhere.")

God's answer to this question came quickly. He told Marilyn to take the verses of Scripture from 1 Timothy 3 that dealt with deacons and elders and to pray these verses, placing Michael's name in them.

She began speaking those things that were not yet a reality as though they were. She daily inserted Michael's name in the verses of Scripture as she prayed.

And Michael changed. He got worse!

Marilyn continued in obedience to God's instruction in spite of how Michael was acting, and then a positive change did begin—but it was in her. She started seeing Michael the way God saw him rather than the way he was.

One day she prayed, "God, if Michael would just go to a Full Gospel Businessmen's meeting . . ."

God said, "No, no, no. See Michael *speaking* at a Full Gospel Businessmen's meeting."

A little later God directed her to begin speaking those same Scriptures with much greater boldness, coming against the evil spirits trying to control her husband's life.

Things continued to change in Marilyn's view of her husband. She became filled with the Word of God's view of him. When he came home drunk at three in the morning (or didn't come home at all), she would say, "That's not like Michael."

Finally, God's love won Michael's heart. He is now what the Scriptures say Godly husbands are to be. Michael and Marilyn's marriage is healed. They now serve as the National Coordinators of Nova Shalom, an arm of Born-Again Marriages that helps couples willing to work to get God's best in their marriages. The marriages range from those that are good and want to get better to those that are on the brink of divorce.

Nova Shalom is a thirteen-week course of "one-flesh" principles that is taught in homes by trained couples. It is mushrooming throughout the nation. Mike and Marilyn and other couples working with them train leader couples who then teach the course in their communities.

Anyone privileged to sit under Michael's anointed teaching witnesses the miracle of the life-changing power of God's Word. It is hard to imagine he was ever anything other than the man of God he now is.

Many people have to make the same choice about their mates that Marilyn had to make—let him follow the will of the flesh and see the devil's plan swallow him up, or, be a partner with God to see His plan come to pass.

God never intended for marriages to be victimized and homes to be raped by the devil, but for too long we Christians have been ignorant of our mighty weapons through God or just too lazy to pick them up and fight.

Some people still say, "Well, if God wants to heal my marriage, He will." They forget that God needs the freedom and authority to work through them to bring their marriages back together.

Realize that you must fight the spiritual battles where your mate is losing.

The easiest thing to do is the last thing your mate needs, that is, to blame and berate him or her for their faults. They may not know what they need. In fact, often the person being beaten by the devil has no knowledge of who he is actually fighting with. It follows then that they also do not know how they are repeatedly falling into the same sin traps.

Up to this point you may have had the same question—"Why isn't that pattern changing?"

The answer is found in Ephesians 6:12: "For we wrestle not against flesh and blood, but against principalities, against powers, against the rulers of the darkness of this world, against spiritual wickedness in high places."

The fact is we are fighting an enemy we can't see. First Peter 5:8 says, "The devil, as a roaring lion, walketh about, seeking whom he may devour."

Your mate is not the problem. Their pills, the bottle, or the lovers aren't the problem. The problem is the evil spirits which enslave them even against their own wills.

How do you fight a battle with enemy spirits you can't see? What are the available weapons?

Matthew 16:19 explains it beautifully: "And I will give unto thee the keys of the kingdom of heaven: and whatsoever thou shalt bind on earth shall be bound in heaven: and whatsoever thou shalt loose on earth shall be loosed in heaven."

The simple but powerful process is to take the name of Jesus and speak to the spirits such as adultery, alcohol, and gambling that are influencing your mate. Command them to stop in the name of Jesus!

It's a scriptural fact that if you don't enforce the law against the devil, God will not do it for you. That's why well-meaning, sincere people can go years without breaking problem patterns from their loved ones. They never stand up spiritually and take their rightful place on behalf of that loved one.

The Mafia is illegal but can operate unless the law is enforced. In the same way, the devil has no right to destroy your family but won't stop unless you exercise your authority.

That authority has been provided to every born-again Christian from Jesus himself. He says, "Behold, I give *you* power to tread on serpents and scorpions (demons), and over all the power of the enemy: and nothing shall by any means hurt you" (Luke 10:19).

First John 3:8, speaking of sin, says, "For this purpose the Son of God was manifested, that he might destroy the works of the devil."

Most often this spiritual warfare is done alone in prayer rather than in the presence of the person you are helping. It works in the spiritual realm totally apart from what their mind consciously knows. Remember, people who are trapped by their habits and problems are not responding to rational thought but rather to spirit influences.

And what about the person's free will?

Kenneth Hagin aptly answers the question in his marvelous book, *The Authority of the Believer*. "We are not governing the person's free will; we are governing the spirits behind their will."

When these foul devils are bound and their voices silenced and the Holy Spirit is authorized to go to work on the sinner, His lovely voice comes through loud and clear. And who can resist the majesty of Jesus?

In difficult marriage situations, using this spiritual warfare is clearly one of the main reasons why some marriages get healed that normally would have turned into divorce statistics.

A mate must also adopt a Godly attitude toward the troubled spouse if the marriage is to healed.

Second Timothy 2:24-25 tells us, "And the servant of the Lord must not strive; but be gentle unto all men, apt to teach, patient, in meekness instructing those that oppose themselves; if God peradventure will give them repentance to the acknowledging of the truth."

Examples of the opposite of the above verses are things like spiritual superiority, pride, arrogance, self-righteous contempt, and especially a critical and judgmental spirit or a "holier than thou" attitude.

As a mate patterns himself after God, he will start believing in his spouse just as God does. Then genuine compassion will be able to help that person come to repentance.

God's attitude is summed up in 2 Corinthians 5:15: "He died for all, that they which live should not henceforth live unto themselves, but unto him which died for them, and rose again." This means we must develop a lifestyle of being like Jesus.

A final way to help a mate who can't seem to help himself is to love in the same way that God loved us.

Jesus gives us an important direction concerning this. "A new commandment I give unto you, That ye love one another; as I have loved you, that ye also love one another" (John 13:34).

Jesus loved His Bride enough to die for Her. This is hard for us to comprehend, but when God's love is in our hearts, we are better able to love unconditionally. Our selfish patterns will have to die if we are going to help a troubled mate. We will have to sacrifice some personal desires to see our hurting mate healed. We will even have to give up the self-pity and attention others have given us because of "all we have to put up with."

As we love our troubled mates in the way Christ loved us

when we were yet in willful sin, we will have a sure reward for our love.

Pattern your life after Jesus—"Looking unto Jesus the author and finisher of our faith; who for the joy that was set before him endured the cross, despising the shame, and is set down at the right hand of the throne of God. For consider him that endured such contradiction of sinners against himself, lest ye be wearied and faint in your minds" (Heb. 12:2-3).

We are now getting to where the rubber meets the road. To say you are a Christian is one thing. But to yield to the Spirit of Jesus is another.

Jesus said, "If any man will come after me, let him deny himself, and take up his cross daily, and follow me. For whosoever will save his life shall lose it: but whosoever will lose his life for my sake, the same shall save it" (Luke 9:23-24).

5

What Can Be Done When A Partner Does Not Care About The Marriage But Does Not Want A Divorce?

My immediate answer is to do everything we've discussed in the preceding chapters and then a little bit more.

In my opinion this situation is one of the roughest marriage problems a partner can face. These kinds of marriages are filled with pretenses. Often relatives, friends, and business associates assume the marriage is normal because the uncommitted partner puts up a great front. But at home, when the couple is alone, the indifference or the quarreling can be unbearable unless the caring partner knows how to aggressively come against these things through prayer.

Sometimes when a mate does not care about the marriage, the spouse is often humiliated and ridiculed in front of the children and sometimes even in public.

The spirits of hate, anger, and bitterness seem to gravitate to this type of situation. It isn't uncommon to hear those spirits speak out of the mouth of the uncommitted spouse in a way that is foreign to how the person normally speaks to anyone else. They say especially ugly things to the marriage partner who is standing for the marriage. Devils motivating people know they are up against the Holy Spirit in the committed mate, so they'll try to wear him down and get him to battle in the flesh instead of in God's power.

From my experience I've seen that it is easier in many ways to pray and "stand" for a person who has moved out than for one who remains at home and gives vent to every vile thing the devil motivates him to do or say.

I am not advocating separation and am not encouraging that alternative. Rather, I want to stress that a person in such a situation must go after all the power God has to offer with every fiber of his being and then use it! And use it . . . and use it until God reigns in that partner's heart and, together, they kick the devil out of their home.

I know many people who are living in absolute victory even though the fire is raging around them. They are like the Hebrew children in the fiery furnace who didn't get burned.

Only by God giving the partner who wants to see the marriage healed the ability to believe for the healing of that relationship can things change. It is a spiritual battle needing spiritual solutions.

What is the first thing a person must do who desires to become a "stander" for the healing of his/her marriage?

When people call Born-Again Marriages for counseling, we ask, "Are you born again?"

Anyone who has not asked Jesus to forgive him of his sins and has not made Jesus the Lord of his life does not stand a chance when it comes to healing a deeply troubled marriage.

Again and again the Word of God shows us our need to invite the Spirit of Jesus into our lives. This, incidentally, is the only way He gets there.

Once a person repents and gives Jesus that simple invitation, he becomes what the Bible refers to in the third chapter of John as "born again" or saved. Jesus says, "Except a man be born again, he cannot see the kingdom of God" (John 3:3).

In verse six He explains what the two births are: "That which is born of the flesh is flesh; and that which is born of the Spirit is spirit." The first birth is of our earthly parents, and the second birth is of our heavenly Father.

Romans 10:8-10 explains that our rebirth is spoken into being:

The word is nigh thee, even in thy mouth, and in thy heart: that is, the word of faith, which we preach; That if thou shalt confess with thy mouth the Lord Jesus, and shalt believe in thine heart that God hath raised him from the dead, thou shalt be saved. For with the heart man believeth unto righteousness; and with the mouth confession is made unto salvation.

The second question we ask those who come to us for counseling is, "Are you baptized in the Holy Spirit?"

Any person who wants to walk victoriously may, but it will be done through releasing the power of the Holy Spirit within him.

The pressures of hell are stronger than your own power but not nearly as strong as the Holy Spirit's power. To have this power in your life, you need only ask for and receive Christ's gift of the Holy Spirit as His followers did on the Day of Pentecost.

The final words Jesus spoke to His disciples before He went back to heaven to be with the Father were directions to be baptized in the Holy Spirit.

"Wait for the promise of the Father," Jesus said, "which ye have heard of me. For John truly baptized with water; but ye shall be baptized with the Holy Spirit" (Acts 1:4-5).

Then Jesus explained the result of the baptism in the Holy Spirit, "Ye shall receive power after that the Holy Spirit is come upon you . . . " (vs.8). If there is anything a person with a troubled marriage needs, it's the power of God at work in their situation. Power to love. Power to forgive. Power to see as God does. Power to live above circumstances. Power to pray God's perfect will down on our mates when we in ourselves "know not how to pray as we ought." Power to thwart the plans of the devil.

The very men Jesus had called to change the world were not to leave town until they received this power from the Holy Spirit in their lives.

Christ's followers gathered for prayer in Jerusalem and waited for the promised power of the Holy Spirit. Acts 2:1-4 describes what happened next:

And when the day of Pentecost was fully come, they were all with one accord in one place. And suddenly there came a sound from heaven as of a rushing mighty wind, and it filled all the house where they were sitting. And there appeared unto them cloven tongues like as of fire, and it sat upon each of them. And they were all filled with the Holy Ghost, and began to speak with other tongues, as the Spirit gave them utterance.

The apostle Peter was one of those baptized in the Holy Spirit that day. Less than two months earlier he had denied three times that he even knew Jesus.

But the day he was baptized in the Holy Spirit, he became a mighty man of God. He preached a sermon to many of the same people who only a few days earlier had screamed at Jesus, "Crucify Him! Crucify Him!" After Peter's brief but power-packed message, 3,000 of them accepted Christ as their Savior.

He and the others now had the power of God's Holy Spirit coming from within their spirits. This was the same power Jesus had told them they had to receive in order to be equipped for their ministry.

Husbands and wives in troubled marriages need the same power of the Holy Spirit to change and heal their marriages.

The Holy Spirit gives a person Divine wisdom to handle critical situations. He gives a marriage partner peace where there seems to be no peace. He gives each person a supernatural prayer language that speaks directly to the Father about problems that trouble people spiritually and emotionally. Sometimes the people do not even know these problems exist and therefore could not express them if they didn't pray in the Spirit.

When you seem to be missing it; when you can't seem to get victory in some area, pray much in the Spirit. Romans 8:27 says that the Holy Spirit knows the mind or the plan of God for you. Interceding in the Spirit will allow the Holy Spirit to pray God's perfect plan into existence for you.

Sometimes as you intercede for your partner, the Holy Spirit within you will begin to weep or groan. You are travailing for your partner. Don't consult your mind at that time; just give the Holy Spirit freedom to pray through you. Paul said in Galatians 4:19, "My little children, I travail in birth for you again until Christ be formed within you."

I encourage you to grow to the maturity of "birthing"

things in the Spirit with deep groanings. Miraculous things happen in the physical after prayer in the Spirit. And troubled marriage partners need Christ formed within them.

After you learn to let your spirit override your mind and yield to the deep groanings needed to "birth" something in the Spirit, you will hardly be able to wait until that time alone with God to "birth" the next project God lays on your heart.

To do battle, the believer is to take on the whole armor of God—which includes His beautiful gift of praying in the Spirit. Ephesians 6:13-18 describes the believer's dress:

> Wherefore take unto you the whole armour of God, that ye may be able to withstand in the evil day, and having done all, to stand. Stand therefore, having your loins girt about with truth, and having on the breastplate of righteousness; and your feet shod with the preparation of the gospel of peace; above all, taking the shield of faith, wherewith ye shall be able to quench *all* the fiery darts of the wicked. And take the helmet of salvation, and the sword of the Spirit, which is the word of God: *Praying always* with all prayer and supplication *in the Spirit* . . .

The Strength Of The One-Flesh Covenant

When two people enter into marriage, a tremendous thing takes place spiritually. There is a spiritual joining that is so complete that even couples who later think they hate each other go through definite trauma when they divorce. Even in earthly terms, this joining puts them in a legal position that if either signs the family name, they are both responsible.

In the same manner, a born-again mate may pray with authority as a representative before God on behalf of their marriage. Either husband or wife also has the right and authority to deal with the devil on behalf of their partner. Many people in bad marriages do not realize that alone they can stand against Satan as a representative of their "one-flesh" covenant.

You are one with your partner, and you can protect your spouse from Satan's vicious attacks and win. You can do great exploits in the Spirit as the covenant representative of that marriage.

We have the right to use the name of Jesus when we pray and when we bind the devil because we are in a covenant relationship with Him. Jesus has given himself to us and we have given ourselves to Him. We are one with Him and He is one with us. We are in Him and He is in us. We are "bone of His bone and flesh of His flesh." What's His is ours and what's ours is His. This is a covenant relationship.

Marriage is the same kind of covenant. God sees you and your covenant marriage partner as being as much made of one flesh as Adam and Eve were. Each wife is as though she were made from her husband's side, and each husband, as though he gave a part of his flesh and bone to create his wife.

In our marriage, when Dru accepted Jesus as her Lord and began praying for me, I was changed. I didn't want to change but it seemed I had no choice in the matter. Something was happening, and I didn't know what it was. Without me have anything to say about it, Dru had gotten born again and in doing so had changed my relationship both with sin and with God.

First Corinthians 7:14 explains what had happened to me

because of what she did: "For the unbelieving husband is sanctified by the wife, and the unbelieving wife is sanctified by the husband."

For me, "the pleasures of sin" days had ended. I even tried to sin more because the sin I was in was not satisfying. But it wouldn't work. I had become "sanctified" by my believing wife. The word, *sanctified*, means to be set apart from a profane use to a holy use.

Because of the spiritual strength of the marriage covenant with my wife established years earlier by our mutual vows, her recent born-again commitment had limited Satan's access to my life. Rather than him having free access to me and God having limited access, Dru's new covenant relationship with Jesus had reversed the roles. Now it was God who had free access and the devil who had limited access. I couldn't find pleasure the way I used to. My sinful life became increasingly empty.

When God said in Malachi 2:14 that He was a witness to the covenant of your marriage, He was saying that marriage *is* a covenant. Furthermore, He was declaring himself to be the third covenant partner to that marriage! He was saying that because marriage is a Divinely ordained covenant, He is an active rather than neutral party to it. He is making the case clear that marriage is a God-caliber relationship, not a mere agreement between humans.

For you who weren't Christians when you were married, the good news is that once you were born again, every promise in the Bible became yours—including Malachi 2:14! When just one marriage partner becomes born again, *the promise in Malachi 2:14 is retroactive*. God being the third witness to your marriage is your covenant right the moment you become born again, and you can know without a shadow of doubt that you have God Almighty as your witness to establish or hold together the covenant of your marriage and not let man put it "asunder."

Once just one of these earth representatives to the marriage covenant recognizes the strength of this covenant, he can stand for the healing of their marriage effectively with faith, knowing he and God are two agreeing witnesses to hold this covenant together in the Spirit. Both Old and New Testaments clearly state it takes two or more witnesses to establish any matter (see Deut. 19:15, Matt. 18:16, 2 Cor. 13:1).

This means that although a divorce may be granted in an earthly court and marital privileges of living together must be abandoned temporarily, it is no big problem to get remarried to your spouse after he has had a heart healing and returns home.

During the writing of this book, I had the great honor of performing my first marriage. It was the happy reuniting of one of our standers and her husband after fifteen months of divorce. The wedding took place at our Born-Again Marriages headquarters with all the local standers' groups present and was like no other marriage anyone had ever attended.

The wife read her favorite verse of Scripture that she stood on for the healing of her marriage. It was Jeremiah 33:11, "[There shall be heard again] the voice of joy and the voice of gladness, the voice of the bridegroom and the voice of the bride, the voices of those who sing as they bring sacrifices of thanksgiving into the house of the Lord, Give praise and thanks to the Lord of hosts, for the Lord is good, for His mercy and kindness and steadfast love endure for ever! For I will cause the captivity of the land (the woman substituted the word, *marriage*) to be reversed and return to be as it was at first, says the Lord" (Amp.).

Acting as witnesses were Dru and Marilyn Conrad, the National Standers' coordinator, who signed the new marriage license—the document of life.

Then the wife read a few lines from the divorce document which had declared that the marriage was "irretrievably broken."

The groom next took a match and burned the divorce papers—the document of death. This was amid happy tears and cheers to Jesus from onlookers. Romans 8:2 declares, "For the law of the Spirit of life in Christ Jesus hath made me free from the law of sin and death."

Let the above example be a faith-builder to those of you who have received or may in the future receive divorce papers prior to the manifested healing of your marriage. Granted, it is a sad and emotional experience to go through a divorce. That decree may look very official and very ominous. But the same God who magnificently reversed man-made decrees that were against His will as recorded in the books of Ezra and Esther is the same God who reversed our newly remarried couple's divorce decree. He will do the same for you! Psalm 112:7 must be in your spirit as it was for this standing wife: "He (she) shall not be afraid of evil tidings: his (her) heart is fixed, trusting in the Lord."

Believe me, those divorce papers looked *very powerless* and fragile in the flames and turned to ashes. Watching one of Satan's works destroyed in front of my eyes reminded me of Isaiah 14:16, which speaks of the day Satan will be bound forever in hell, and we'll all look upon him and say, "Is this the man that made the earth to tremble, that did shake kingdoms?"

As the fire quickly did its work, we could say, "Devil, is that the decree that was supposed to make this believing wife tremble?

6

What Can Be Done When The Partner Who Does Not Want The Marriage To Work Has Filed For Divorce?

When a marriage partner is faced with these "final"-type situations, it can look as though there is little or nothing left to do. The truth is that some of the highest quality work that God does in people's lives is at the point of their greatest obstacle.

It is not that God has chosen to wait before giving His very best. Rather, it's because people usually don't give God their full attention until a crisis hits. When our backs are against the wall, our attitude toward obeying God changes.

When things really look impossible, people begin saying things such as, "Anything You say, Father, I'll do." They stop thinking they can handle it themselves. Finally, they are genuinely open to hearing what God has to say.

The greatest thing persons whose mates have filed for divorce can do is look to the Word for their answers.

Too often people look at circumstances rather than to God.

First John 5:14-15 says, "And this is the confidence that we have in him, that, if we ask anything according to his will, he heareth us: and if we know that he hear us, whatsoever we ask, we know that we have the petitions that we desired of him."

And we know God's will is for your marriage to work. In fact, we hear God's perfect will for marriage at every wedding we attend: "What therefore God hath joined together, let not man put asunder" (Matt. 19:6).

Every believing mate can be as excited as Dru was when on the day she was born again, Lee and Carolyn shared those two verses with her. She discovered the spiritual fact that because her prayer for our marriage to be healed was according to God's will, God had granted her petition the moment she prayed, believed she'd received, and thanked Him for it.

Second Corinthians 4:18 says, "We look not at the things which are seen (such as a crumbling marriage), but at the things that are not seen: for the things which are seen are temporal (subject to change); but the things which are not seen are eternal."

Believers have new eyes. They see things as God sees them. A believer's policy must be, "I walk by faith, not by sight," as 2 Corinthians 5:7 says. Believers cannot afford to listen to "doubting Thomases" who don't believe the marriage can be healed.

As a Christian mate walks by faith, he stays single-minded. James 1:8 warns, "A double-minded man is unstable in all his ways." The Christian can choose to believe God or to believe circumstances. Circumstances change, but *God's Word doesn't*.

God begins working on a spouse's heart the instant the believing mate begins praying. The spouse may not act or talk any differently, but the believing mate is not limited to looking at circumstances anymore.

Many times pride will not allow the rebellious partner to tell you who are praying all the thoughts he is having or how many Christians are coming in his path every day. But some day that mate will tell you and thank you for having stood in the gap.

You must *know* God is doing these things by *faith* because of your intercession.

It has been ten years since Dru prayed me home, and every now and then while doing a seminar, something will come to mind that God did during my time away from home. And as I tell the people, Dru will say, "You never told me about that one!" and she'll get to thank Jesus all over again right there in front of our audience.

Many times a person wanting a divorce will flaunt his sins. While the rebellious partner is flaunting his sins, the partner who is standing for the marriage healing must humble himself. James 4:6 says, "God resisteth the proud, but giveth grace to the humble." To eliminate any doubt as to how serious God is about this principle, it is repeated in Matthew 23:12 and 1 Peter 5:6.

In simple terms, going against God is the epitome of pride, and doing the Father's pleasure is the essence of being humble.

If you take God at His word, which you must do, it becomes extremely simple to have faith for the desired outcome. I mean simple! The proud is coming down while the humble is being exalted. Somewhere in the process of these two operations is an inevitable point where the proud sees clearly the error of his ways. At that point, the humble is in position to receive a harvest.

Humble partners must stay tender before the Lord and never let arrogance, religious pride, spiritual superiority, or self-righteousness take root. If humility departs from the standing partner, the marriage will have no base for restoration.

Philippians 2:5-9 says,

Let this same attitude and purpose and [humble] mind be in you which was in Christ Jesus.—Let Him be your example in humility—Who, although being essentially one with God and in the form of God [possessing the fullness of the attributes which make God God], did not think this equality with God was a thing to be eagerly grasped or retained; But stripped Himself [of all privileges and rightful dignity] so as to assume the guise of a servant (slave), in that He became like men and was born a human being. And after He had appeared in human form He abased and humbled Himself [still further] and carried His obedience to the extreme of death, even the death of [the] cross! Therefore [because He stooped so low], God has highly exalted Him and has freely bestowed on Him the name that is above every name . . . (Amp.).

Verses 13-16 expand the thought:

[Not in your own strength] for it is God Who is all the while effectually at work in you—energizing and creating in you the power and desire—both to will and to work for His good pleasure and satisfaction and delight. (Note: And God is delighted to see you standing for the healing of your marriage!)

Do all things without grumbling and faultfinding and complaining [against God] and questioning and doubting [among yourselves], That you may show yourselves to be blameless and guileless, innocent and uncontaminated, children of God without blemish (faultless, unrebukable) in the midst of a crooked and wicked generation— [spiritually] perverted and perverse (that is, partners in adultery, etc.). *Among whom you are seen as bright lights—stars or beacons shining out clearly—in the [dark] world*; Holding out [to it] and offering [to all men] the Word of Life... (Amp.).

One of the most asked questions about this type of marriage healing is, *"How long will it take?"*

At Born-Again Marriages we have seen unbelieving spouses change directions the same day their mates accepted Jesus into their lives. In most cases, however, it takes longer. But *when you are prepared to wait forever, it doesn't take very long.*

One of the major things most people who want their marriage healed need to work on at this point is to learn how Jesus can make them happy. He wants to be our source of peace, joy, wisdom, fulfillment, love, and everything else we need. He is able to be all of this to us.

The fact is that most partners start looking to the marriage healing for their happiness. However, when they let Jesus become their happiness, they are taking a major step toward a healed marriage.

If Jesus who is God Almighty can't make you happy, what chance does your partner who is a mere human have?

Jesus' peace does not automatically reign in our hearts. God says He will draw near to you *if* you draw near to Him (James 4:8). If you want Jesus to fulfill you, He must be your number one priority. TV and bowling will not meet your needs during times of loneliness or trials. Being in the Word, praying MUCH in the Spirit, and then just plain pouring out your heart in quiet times to Jesus will give you peace in spite of some of the difficult circumstances that you face.

Dru and I know hundreds of spouses who have learned to hear the voice of Jesus for their wisdom and have become strong Christians while praying their partners home. They now have powerful ministries for the Lord. They are not just trying to "hang on" or "cope." They are thrilled with the life Jesus has given them. They have reached a point of maturity with Jesus they never thought possible. This is your goal: "Seek ye first the kingdom of God, and his righteousness; and all these things shall be added unto you" (Matt. 6:33).

As the born-again spouse waits for the marriage to be healed, he can also listen to the Lord on how to get his own spiritual life in order.

Usually marriage problems have their roots in abuses by both spouses. The one who wants healing *must* mature in the Lord. God will not manifest the prayer for a healed marriage before you are ready to handle it.

In the process of praying and standing for someone who thinks they want out, there is an enormous spiritual gulf between their position and yours.

One thing you must remember is that you aren't fighting *against* your spouse; you're fighting *for* him. The battle is against the devil. This is especially important to know because the mate for whom you are standing will be so sure you're against him that if you're not careful, he'll convince you. The troubled spouse will say things such as, "If you really loved me, you'd let me go."

Frankly, if you take your eyes off God's Word and lose sight of the fact that there is a right and wrong, you will begin to lose your confidence. It's almost impossible for a spouse to understand where you are really "coming from" until God's work is completed in his heart.

Wayward spouses are blinded by their present deception. Second Corinthians 4:4 says, "In whom the god of this world hath blinded the minds of them which believe not, lest the light of the glorious gospel of Christ, who is the image of God, should shine unto them."

A spouse who believes divorce is his only way out of his problems is like a man on a bridge about to jump and commit suicide. When people see the person about to jump, they mobilize their forces to save his life. The suicidal person thinks everyone is against him. The fact is everyone is for him, trying to save his life.

It's like rescuing an animal caught in a trap. Because the animal is in so much pain, it usually mistakes the rescuer for the enemy.

When a hurting mate lashes out against you, his praying partner, you must react with compassion.

Hurting marriage partners, even those filing for a divorce, are hungry for something that will work. God's love working through a spiritual mate will make a permanent impact on that hurting person's life and desires. Only intercession and spiritual warfare done diligently in that person's behalf will force the devil's blinders off his heart and mind and bring him out of darkness. Unselfish intercession is truly the God-kind of love in action.

By now you have noticed that there are many scripturally sound principles I am encouraging you to apply regardless of the state of your marriage. In addition, we have discussed things not to do. A point I want you to understand is that *making a mistake doesn't blow you out of the ball game*. Things such as avoiding strife, loving unconditionally, and walking in forgiveness are developed abilities.

One couple we worked with was separated, and the husband desired with all his heart to see his wife and child return. He was applying the various principles quite well, but one of the problems in their marriage had been his temper. Again and again he had done things that he later regretted; his wife turned to someone else.

He had repented and asked God to forgive him. Knowing that his temper had been a major source of their trouble, he put up his guard against it.

He was doing very well even in the face of the hurt of his wife being with another man—that is, until one night when he let his guard down. He said a little too much to her and let the old temper have its full sway.

Before he knew what had happened, he hit his wife!

It seemed that all his hard work had just gone down the drain. He called me on the phone, heartbroken, and with sobs blurted out, "I just slapped my wife in the face! Now God *can't* heal my marriage!"

My reply was, "Shut up, devil!" I began praying for him and helped him again to receive God's forgiveness.

Once more he girded up his determination and said, "Temper, you have to go in Jesus' name. You cannot have me!" Together we picked up the pieces and began thanking God for healing their marriage.

Naturally speaking, that event just confirmed to his wife that she was better off without him.

With God on our side, we are not dealing with the limitations of the natural realm. We accept the fact that it's going to take a miracle from God and then go for the miracle.

Was their marriage healed? Yes! How did it happen? Believe me, it *was* a miracle. The very next time I had a call from him, they were on the line together, giggling and giving praises to God.

Had there been a time span? Yes, but he knew what to do with it. He strengthened himself in the Word of God and in prayer. He spent much time praying for his wife and keeping his confidence in God high pertaining to her.

Today, seven years later, every time we see them, they say they are still on their honeymoon. They have a second child—a beautiful three-and-one-half-year-old girl. Their healed marriage is a bright light beaming the message, "Don't let discouragement, setbacks, or mistakes keep you from your dream!"

We strive for perfection, but God's grace covers our mistakes.

Another very crucial thing to remember is this: Do not expect partners who are in rebellion to God to act like Christians!

They may very well be born-again, Spirit-baptized believers, but . . . if they are bent on divorce or are in adultery or some other sin, they are listening to and obeying the wrong spirit. The devil, the father of lies, is influencing them, and they will act like him.

Understand there could even be some temporary insanity, and you won't be caught off guard if it happens. Just realize people listening to devils act like devils, and the devil has no sense of justice or mercy. In fact, the devil is crazy. Only the name of Jesus used in unrelenting spiritual warfare stops sinners from acting like devils.

If you are yielded to God and determined to love your partner unconditionally and bind the devil off him or her, then *you* are the one God expects to act like Jesus would act—whether that partner deserves it or not. You may slip a few times at first, but as you mature in Christ and your flesh gets crucified, you won't be emotionally stunned by some devilish outburst from your partner; you'll merely recognize a devil when you see one, go to your prayer closet, and send it fleeing from you in the name of Jesus.

We limit God when we judge things from our own perspective rather than from God's. I am convinced that the perspective it takes to win can come only from God.

Some Christians are like the Israelites who only looked at natural circumstances just before David battled Goliath. Some Christians say, "With God all things are possible—except in marriage problems." It's because that giant just looks too big for them. The good news is that the person with God has the winner's edge. There are no exceptions with God. He has no limitations.

A woman in Columbus, Ohio, didn't limit God. Her marriage had already broken up before she accepted Jesus as her Savior. Her husband was involved in crime and living an extremely immoral lifestyle.

After being born again, she began reading the Bible and discovered God's desire for marriages to be healed.

As she prayed and read the Word, God revealed to her that He would heal her marriage. She waited, expecting her husband to have a change of heart.

Instead, he proceeded to file for and obtain a divorce. She could not understand what was happening but continued to believe what God had shown her.

Then her husband remarried. "I must have heard God wrong," she thought.

"But, God, I know You promised to heal my marriage. How could this be happening and Your promise to me still be true? I know I heard You," she prayed.

At this point, had she been following what some person taught her, she would have been on real shaky ground. But she knew God had spoken to her. She continued to read her Bible and pray and thank God for the healing. There were more questions inside her than answers, so she simply stayed before God with an attitude that He would direct her.

Some might say that at this point she moved from being the "wronged" one to being the "wrong" one—that she should not stay true to him, that she should not expect his return. She should face the facts and make a new life for herself. And she should respect the fact that a new marriage ceremony had taken place.

But would it be right before God for her to respect the new marriage vows when in doing so it meant disrespecting her own? When as a young woman she said, "I *will* be true to you until death do us part," she meant it. Should she now say she was wrong to have meant every word of that vow she had made before God years before? Is there a heavenly response to a rare breed of covenant keepers, as Ecclesiastes 5:1-6 says?

Is 1 Corinthians 7:15, "If the unbelieving depart, let him depart," a spiritual "copout"? When you have God's will in Matthew 19:6 and Mark 10:9, "What God hath joined together let not man put asunder," and you're praying according to God's will, it merely means if he departs, you may have to let him go physically for a time, but by no means does it say you can't pray him back home again.

Is there any connection between the over-all scriptural teaching on forgiveness and, more specifically, Jesus' forgiveness of the woman caught in adultery in John 8?

My friend in Ohio forgave her husband both of committing adultery while being married to her and also of marrying another woman—which Matthew 19:9, Mark 10:11, and Luke 16:18 say is also adultery.

Does the fact that Jesus redeemed believers from the curse of the law (Gal. 3:3) and the fact that adultery is under the curse (Deut. 28:30—"Thou shalt betroth a wife and another man shall lie with her") give her a spiritual legality with which she can rescue her husband?

Many believers know Jesus redeemed us from the curse of poverty and sickness. But Jesus also redeemed your marriage from the curse of adultery. Once you believe that fact, the spirit of adultery can no longer run roughshod over your marriage and the thief cannot steal your marriage partner from you.

Those who would say she is wrong in wanting him back would use Deuteronomy 24:1-3 for support. Yet, when God referred to that text in Jeremiah 3, He not only invited Israel who was married to other gods to come back to Him, He boldly stated, "I am married to you" (Jer.3:14).

Jeremiah 3:12 declares true repentance would stop God's anger from falling upon them for the sin of Deuteronomy 24. Today, true repentance causes the blood of Jesus to cleanse us from *all* sins, including that of Deuteronomy 24.

In Ohio, this lady did not know anyone who would give her any encouragement. So she didn't say much to anyone. Even though she thought she knew it was God who had assured her of the healing, she was confused and discouraged. Knowing her only hope was in God, she kept praying and reading the Word.

One day she read Ezra, and in chapters nine and ten she got the encouragement she needed. There she found the story of 113 men who had taken strange wives. In this true story, because of the intercessory prayers of Ezra, the priest, God told all these men to put away their strange wives even though they had children born to the marriages.

When she saw that, she was ecstatic. Her confidence in

receiving her promise from God went sky high. She knew that she knew that somehow God would get her husband out of crime and away from the other woman and back home where he belonged.

During this time, he had a monthly bill at his local bar of $1,600. One day as she prayed, God told her not to see him as that kind of man but rather to envision him preaching the gospel, to see him in a pulpit.

A period of time went by in which she grew tremendously in her relationship with the Lord. Then one day in prayer the Spirit of God gave her a hair-raising instruction. Her husband had become homesick for his little girls, and God told her to move out and give him the home and authority over the girls.

She struggled with the decision but decided to trust God.

Two weeks after her decision, her husband broke. The great love his wife demonstrated overcame his selfishness.

He accepted Jesus into his life and changed dramatically. He divorced the other woman. Then he remarried the mother of his children. He gave up his criminal activities and reformed.

Recently I was in Columbus, conducting a marriage seminar. This husband and wife were there also, and with them were couples from all over Ohio. Not only has their marriage been healed, but people all around them whose lives they have touched are also receiving healed marriages.

All this happened because a wife had kept her eyes on God's promise and did as He said instead of looking at circumstances.

Incidentally, remember that pulpit God told her to picture her husband in? He's now ordained and has preached from that very spot. If God be for us, who can be against us?

Is It Ever God's Desire For A Couple To Divorce?

Other than the Ezra 9 account which I discussed earlier, I have never found a passage in the Bible where God says, "Thus saith the Lord, 'Get a divorce.'" Never have I seen a passage of Scripture written by the apostle Paul or any other of God's representatives that advocates getting a divorce.

Many people try to justify their actions by using any Bible verse they can. They often already have their minds made up on the subject and now simply want God's Word to confirm their decisions.

I don't believe people who advocate divorce have scriptural precedent. The fact is, I know they don't. As clear as the Word of God is on the subject, you have to have help to misunderstand it.

When the Pharisees asked Jesus about divorce, He quickly answered, "Have ye not read, that he which made them at the beginning made them male and female, and said, 'For this cause shall a man leave father and mother, and shall cleave to his wife: and they twain shall be one flesh'? Wherefore they are no more twain, but one flesh. What therefore God hath joined together, let not man put asunder" (Matt. 19:4-6).

In working to heal marriages, Dru and I frequently hear the supposedly scriptural excuses people use for getting divorced. One of the favorites is, "God didn't join us." Others say, "It was lust."

A simple study of "what God hath joined" from Matthew 19 or Mark 10 will show the passages of Scripture to be referring to the spiritual fusing of a couple rather than who or what circumstances brought them to the point of marriage. It is stating God's participation during the wedding vows, not the courtship. It is the act of making the two one flesh, not the selection of which two should be one flesh. God allows us a choice and then backs up that choice.

These verses of Scripture must not be twisted but taken as Jesus' solemn warning that no one should pull married people apart. From the very beginning of creation, God's plan was for man and wife to be one—never to separate.

The Pharisees asked Jesus another question, "Why did Moses then command to give a writing of divorcement, and to put her away?" (vs. 7).

Many people today ask the same type of question, hoping for God's approval of divorce.

Jesus replied, "Moses, *because of the hardness of your hearts*, suffered you to put away your wives: but from the beginning it was not so" (vs. 8). From the beginning of creation divorce was not in God's plan. Divorce because of the hardness of men's hearts—the inability to love unconditionally, the lack of life-long commitment—is another result of the fall of man.

People whose hearts are hardened look for a way out of the marriage vows. There is much discussion over the above verse, but one thing is clear: the Mosaic law that Jesus cited illustrates God's grace, not His desire. God was not advocating divorce. Instead, He allowed Moses to bring some order to a spiritually unregenerated Jewish society that was already commiting acts contrary to God's desire.

Before Moses' instructions were given, Jewish custom held that a man could divorce his wife by simply saying, "I divorce you. I divorce you. I divorce you." He would then throw her and her belongings out of the house. A man in a bad mood could simply have a temper tantrum, blame his wife for something minor, and kick her out.

A degenerated society had lost sight of the sanctity of marriage. In order to force these spiritually hard-hearted Jews to consider the seriousness of divorce, God instructed Moses to enforce a law, having them draw up a written divorce decree and bring it before the Court to make it legal. It also granted some protection to the wife by forcing the husband to give her back her dowry which she had received from her father at the time of betrothal.

A law was also enacted in which the husband paid the girl's father an agreed sum of money called "the bride price." It was put in a special account; and in the contract written at the time of betrothal the husband agreed to give her this money if he ever divorced her. God saw to it that in a patriarchal society, wives could no longer be thrown penniless into the street.

The way God had to deal with spiritually-dead Israel is a far cry from how He expects us as born-again Christians to act when we have the nature of God in our hearts.

God understands marriage better than all of us do. His plan from the creation of the world was for mankind to have fellowship and union with Him. In Jeremiah 3:14 He declares to Israel, "I am married to you."

God knows what it is like to be rejected by those He loves so dearly.

Time after time Israel committed adultery, following other gods. Yet God continually called His Bride back to Him. He promised forgiveness and blessings if she would acknowledge her sins.

But Israel chose her own way.

Jeremiah 3:6-7 records Israel's ways and God's response. "Israel is gone up upon every high mountain and under every green tree, and there hath played the harlot. And I said after she had done all these things, 'Turn thou unto me.' But she returned not."

God declares what He finally had to do to Israel: "I had put her away, and given her a bill of divorce" (vs. 8).

For a long time Dru and I pondered how God could say in Malachi 2:16 that He hated divorce when He himself had given a bill of divorcement to Israel.

One day as Dru and I sat on our sofa in our home, I asked God, "Why did You divorce Israel?"

I was not prepared for the answer.

Within me I began sensing the great grief and agony God suffered because of Israel's unfaithfulness.

I started weeping convulsively. Then God spoke to my heart. I was weeping so hard that I couldn't speak out what He was telling me. Dru brought me a pencil and paper, and I wrote down the thoughts.

God revealed His heart to me as He watched His precious Bride, Israel, go through hell after hell when down through the centuries every demonic world leader tried to annihilate her.

I felt God's pain as she was raped and tortured and led to the gas chambers. All the time, God stood with His arms outstretched to help her, but she wouldn't come under His protection. Israel had broken her marriage covenant to God.

At this point, some of the knowledge we had gleaned from an entire summer's study of ancient Jewish history books and antiquities came flooding to mind.

We learned that the Jews *lived* not only by Mosaic Law but made up many laws of their own which they obeyed as religiously. One of these manmade laws was what the Jews called, "the Law of Defilement." They knew from Jeremiah 3:1,3,9 and many other passages of Scripture, AND from experience, that adultery (either spiritual or physical) committed by their tribe resulted in their land being defiled. This brought drought, plagues, and pestilences. The people greatly feared this defilement coming upon them.

In order to protect the righteous people, the lawyers enacted a law which *forced* any husband whose wife was known to be committing open adultery to give her a writing of divorcement.

Of course, we know in the beginning of Mosaic Law, adulteresses were stoned. However, in Hosea 4:14 God said, "I will not punish your daughters when they play the harlot, nor your daughters-in-law when they commit adultery, for [the fathers and husbands] themselves go aside in order to be alone with women who prostitute themselves for gain, and they sacrifice at the altar with dedicated harlots . . . " (Amp.). So, obviously, stoning gave way to divorce down through the years.

The history books told us that even though the husband of a known adulteress might wish to forgive her and keep her as his wife, he could not! He was literally forced by the local court to divorce her to keep defilement from coming upon the entire tribe.

The point is that adulterous Israel walked out from the covenant protection of her Husband, God.

Jeremiah 3:20 says, "Surely, as a wife treacherously and faithlessly departs from her husband, so have you dealt treacherously and faithlessly with Me, O house of Israel, says the Lord" (Amp.).

Israel left God and practiced spiritual adultery. Even though He wished to forgive her, I believe He could not allow Israel to have one set of rules in human affairs but "play games" in their relationship with Him.

I am convinced God was forced to give Israel a bill of divorcement by their own standards.

God told the Israelites through the prophet Isaiah, "Behold, for your iniquities have ye sold yourselves, and for your transgressions is your mother put away" (Isa. 50:1).

Jeremiah 3:7 records how God begged Israel to repent and turn again to Him, but she would not. Repentance for the sin which broke their covenant was the only way back into the covenant.

Israel divorced herself from God, and she knew it.

God laments in Jeremiah 3:8, "I *had* to put her away and give her a bill of divorcement . . ."

Then God showed me a marvelous thing. He is the original "Stander"! He is standing in faith for the return of His Bride, Israel. Even though there's been a divorce, He says in Jeremiah 3:14, "Turn, O backsliding children, saith the Lord, for I AM MARRIED to you."

God speaks out His faith stand for the healing of His "impossible" marriage in Hosea 2:6-7:

Behold, I, [the Lord God,] will hedge up her way, even yours, [O Israel,] with thorns; and I will build a wall against her, that she shall not find her paths. And she shall follow after her lovers, but she shall not overtake them; and she shall seek them, inquiring for and requiring them, but shall not find them. Then shall she say, Let me go and return to my first husband, for then was it better with me than now (Amp.).

Verse 14 continues, "Therefore, behold, I will allure her [Israel] and bring her into the wilderness, and I will speak tenderly and to her heart" (Amp.). Verse 15 says, "And she shall sing there and respond as in the days of her youth . . ." (Amp.).

Then in verses 16, 19, and 20 God triumphantly declares,

"And it shall be in that day, says the Lord, that you will call Me, My Husband. And I will betroth you to Me forever; yes, I will betroth you to Me in righteousness and justice, and in steadfast love, and in mercies. I will even betroth you to Me in stability and in faithfulness, and you shall know—recognize, be acquainted with, appreciate, give heed to and cherish—the Lord" (Amp.).

(And you who would stand for your marriage would do well to speak God's very own faith-filled words for His Bride over your marriage partner.)

That day as my awesome experience of feeling the heart-throb of God for His rebellious and suffering Bride came to a close, He said to me, "She's coming home to Me with her whole heart; My Son's Bride is going to bring Israel home to Me."

I began to understand why so many Christians continually feel drawn to travel to Israel. God has placed a special love in Christians' hearts toward the Jewish people. And as wave after wave of Christians visit the land and love and pray for the Jews to accept Jesus as their Messiah, Israel's heart is being melted toward God, her faithful Husband.

Does Adultery Break The Marriage Covenant?

Years ago Dru asked God this question because so many theologians advocate divorce if there has been adultery. She knew that in our case adultery had been committed by both of us and yet God healed our marriage. God's Spirit spoke to her very clearly and said: "Adultery is a breach of the marriage contract but is not irreparable."

The Bible bears this out. The Israelites committed spiritual adultery time after time, yet God still renewed the covenant every time they repented from their hearts.

What actually threatens the marriage covenant is not the act of adultery but that of rejecting the person because of it. In the Bible that rejection is called *unforgiveness*.

As a wounded marriage partner "throws in the towel," giving up on the marriage, what he actually is doing is a glaring manifestation of returning evil for evil. He is responding contrary to Romans 12:21 to not be overcome "of evil, but overcome evil with good."

Selfishness would say, "I deserve better," while compassion says, "Father, how can I help?"

I am not implying that adultery is a minor problem. It is extremely serious. It can take people to hell. That is why its victims must be rescued rather than discarded. We are to react the same way Jesus did when the Pharisees brought to Him the woman caught in the very act of adultery. They wanted to stone her; Jesus forgave her of her sin even though He did not sanction it.

In light of Ephesians 5:1-2 where we are asked to be followers of God and "walk in love," do you suppose God is saying, "Write the jerk off"? Do you perceive God saying, "If they wrong you, dispose of them"?

A reading of Matthew 19:9 gives us further New Testament perspective:

And I say unto you, Whosoever shall put away his wife, except it be for fornication, and shall marry another, committeth adultery: and whoso marrieth her which is put away doth commit adultery.

Here Jesus is plainly making a definition of what He considers adultery to be. He does it for the benefit of the hard-hearted Pharisees who were thinking in terms of the Law in which Moses allowed divorce (Deut. 24:1).

History tells us the Jews had so watered down and misinterpreted the Law as to make divorce possible for any cause whatsoever. Ancient Hebrew divorce decrees show men putting away their wives for many frivolous reasons such as careless seasoning of food, going into the street with uncombed hair, talking too much, or even the husband finding a woman more beautiful than his present wife.

You must also remember that because of the hardness of their hearts, God even allowed men to have more than one wife. In this patriarchal society, then, men's definition of adultery was only if they had sexual intercourse with another man's wife. Even going in to a harlot, who was no man's "property," was not considered adultery.

You can imagine the anger of the Pharisees toward Jesus who was putting an end to their "sexual heyday."

All of a sudden these men who regarded wives as property were being told that Jesus was restoring *creation morality*. God expected them to have one wife, and anything other than fidelity to her was now considered adultery by God. No wonder they wanted to stone Jesus.

Jesus was not commanding the Christian whose spouse has committed adultery to get a divorce. He was making a New Covenant definition of adultery. By balancing verses of Scripture with other verses, you will discover that Jesus plainly demonstrated a higher spiritual law—forgiveness.

Forgiveness must become our lifestyle. It is easier to forgive a partner who has committed adultery once than to forgive someone who continues in adulterous relationships.

We often have a shallow view of forgiveness. We are willing to forgive a repentant person. However, our forgiveness does not extend to the person who has not yet acknowledged his error.

We do not realize the extreme importance of forgiveness. A person who forgives a marriage partner for *any* and *all* acts limits Satan's access to that sinning partner. It becomes more difficult for Satan to hold the person in the wrong conduct because, according to Matthew 18:18-22, we are not "binding" them to their sins. When we forgive, we "loose" the sin hold on them, and no longer is any unforgiveness on *our* part blocking God from answering our prayers and working to change the partners' hearts.

John 20:23 says, "Whose soever sins ye remit, they are remitted unto them; and whose soever sins ye retain, they are retained." A marriage partner plays a key role in freeing a partner from sinful ways.

You Have Been Given The Ministry Of Reconciliation

Jesus died for every person; He knew love could change anyone. Second Corinthians 5:17 says, "Therefore if any person is (ingrafted) in Christ, the Messiah, he is (a new creature altogether,) a new creation; the old (previous moral and spiritual condition) has passed away. Behold, the fresh and new has come!" (Amp.).

God can turn old marriage partners into new creations so that divorce does not have to be final.

Malachi 2:16-17 leaves no doubt about God's thoughts concerning divorce:

The Lord, the God of Israel, says: "I hate divorce and marital separation, and him who covers his garment [his wife] with violence. Therefore keep a watch upon your spirit [that it may be controlled by My Spirit], that you deal not treacherously and faithlessly [with your marriage mate]. You have wearied the Lord with your words. Yet you say, 'In what way have we wearied Him?' [You do it when by your actions] you say, 'Every one who does evil is good in the sight of the Lord'" (Amp.).

At the end of the Old Testament God declares, "Behold, I will send you Elijah the prophet . . . , and he shall turn the heart of the fathers to the children, and the heart of the children to their fathers" (Mal. 4:4-5).

God is for healed relationships; He is for reconciliation.

In the New Testament He commissions Christians everywhere to be "ministers of reconciliation" also. Second Corinthians 5:18 says, "All things are of God, who hath reconciled us to himself by Jesus Christ, and hath given to us the ministry of reconciliation."

Jesus reveres the marriage covenant so highly that He suffered and died in order to have His future Bride. He knew the marriage union was worth the pain. When He rose from the dead, He made it possible for us to be born again and become His Bride. Consider this: Jesus didn't have a Bride until He gave all of himself for Her.

Some people think that because something bad doesn't immediately happen to people who are sinning, God is accepting what they do. God loves people, but He doesn't always like what they are doing.

We shouldn't assume that people don't suffer for their actions when we don't see immediate punishment.

Jesus said the wheat and the tares would grow side by

side "until the harvest: and in the time of harvest I will say to the reapers, 'Gather ye together first the tares, and bind them in bundles to burn them, but gather the wheat into my barn'" (Matt. 13:30).

There is a time of judgment coming. Because sinners don't immediately suffer consequences for wrong actions does not mean they won't pay a high price for those deeds in the future. Galatians 6:7-8 declares, "Be not deceived; God is not mocked: for whatsoever a man soweth, that shall he also reap. For he that soweth to his flesh shall of the flesh reap corruption; but he that soweth to the Spirit shall of the Spirit reap life everlasting."

Romans 2:2 says, "But we know that the judgment of God falls justly and in accordance with truth upon those who practice such things" (Amp.).

And verse 4 continues, "Or are you [so blind as] to trifle with and presume upon and despise and underestimate the wealth of His kindness and forbearance and long-enduring patience? Are you unmindful or actually ignorant [of the fact] that God's kindness is intended to lead you to repent— to change your mind and inner man to accept God's will?" (Amp.).

I'll never forget the day I was driving along about six months after I was born again, and the Spirit of God spoke to me and said, "You are not reaping destruction anymore."

Intercessory prayer had caused me to repent and pray for "crop failure" for all the bad seeds I had sown in the past. I had begun sowing Godly seeds.

What if an adulterous mate presumes to be a Christian?

In a strange sort of way this can confuse a Christian spouse. Yet the principles remain basically the same. Just because your mate should "know better" doesn't justify abandoning him.

The mate may or may not be born again. If he is, there is no guarantee that if he lets down his guard and stops reading the Word and praying, he will not fall to Satan's devices.

No matter what, our Godly reaction is to fight the devils off of him. Romans 15:1 says, "We then that are strong ought to bear the infirmities of the weak, and not to please ourselves."

Sometimes it is only intercessory prayer by a dedicated mate, taking the salvation of their sinning mate as their ministry, that saves that partner from hell for eternity. I just know Jesus has special crowns waiting for such as these.

What about yesterday's divorce?

Some people who have committed the sin of divorce continue to justify their actions. As long as they continue pretending it was not wrong, they have not received the forgiveness available to them.

Many people who were divorced and remarried continue to rationalize their past. Sometimes they blame their former mates; sometimes they blame their youthful immaturity at the time of their marriages. They justify their actions, ignoring God's feeling toward divorce and remarriage.

People in second, third, or fourth marriages must stop justifying themselves. They must call their divorces sin and repent so they can be forgiven and go on to receive God's blessing in their present marriage.

Any person who confesses his sin and genuinely repents will be forgiven. I do not mean to merely parrot some words. So many have been suckered by the devil into getting a divorce that it is far too easy to say, "It can't be so bad.

Look at all the people who have done it."

Rationalization and repentance don't mix. Once human logic is set aside and a Godly attitude is released, true repentance can be experienced. Forget about anyone else you know who justifies divorce and start dealing with yourself.

When you say from your heart you're sorry, God washes the slate clean because His Son died for sinners: "Lord, I'm sorry for my part in the divorce. I ask You to forgive me for everything I did wrong that contributed to it."

After a person has repented and received forgiveness for himself, he must then forgive any other persons involved in the deterioration of the marriage. Your partner must be forgiven as well as any third parties who were in adulterous relationships with your mate. Forgive people who gave you bad advice or people who could have helped but didn't know how. Even attorneys who aided in the divorce proceedings must be forgiven.

If, as you read this, you do not feel thoroughly cleansed and forgiven by God, then the ability to forgive others may seem completely out of reach.

Perhaps you want to appropriate the power of God to heal a difficult situation that you are going through right now, but the faith to do so is still beyond your grasp. You may have picked up this book which so openly speaks of God, the Bible, and Jesus; yet, you're aware that you've never been that knowledgeable about spiritual things.

You could be one of so many who've gone to church all their lives but never actually committed your life to Jesus. You're not sure if His Holy Spirit has ever come to live in your heart.

If what you have read has stirred a hunger within you to know God better and to walk your life with Him or if you knew God at one time and have fallen out of fellowship with Him, I would like you to pray the following prayer and sign your name to it.

> *Lord God, in Jesus' name I need to be forgiven. I need Your power in me to forgive others. I see the wrong patterns of my life and ask that You help me to establish new and Godly ones.*
>
> *I open my life to You, Jesus, and invite Your Holy Spirit to live in me and to speak through me. I believe, Jesus, that You did die on a cross and that You did rise from the dead. I now make You my Lord.*
>
> *I give You control of my life. Please give me a hunger to read Your Word and wisdom to understand it. In Jesus' name I denounce Satan and everything demonic and receive God's life in me. I thank You that I am now a born-again Christian. I am a child of the living God. Praise You, Jesus.*

_____   _____

Name   Date

Any person who repents and then prays forgiveness for others will walk in new liberty. Satan no longer has a hold on the person's life, and habitual sin patterns will change. The person no longer feels the need to justify his past; he will not have a "chip" on his shoulder.

Then that person can also become an agent of healing in others' lives. He can say with authority to people in troubled marriages, "God's will is for your marriage to be whole. The divorce that happened to me does not have to happen to you. Let me show you from God's Word how to stop

Satan's destruction in your marriage."

A person who goes through life rationalizing his actions will be helping other people to rationalize their actions. But a person who calls his divorce sin and seeks God's forgiveness will be accepted by Jesus as though he had never sinned. He can be pure before God and help others stay pure also.

Having a second, third, and fourth marriage is wrong. God hates divorce. It is sin. But God's forgiveness does exist! No one can change the past, but it can be forgiven. The divorced person who receives God's forgiveness can go on in life, serving the Lord in a productive and deeply satisfying way and have the blessings of the Lord if he is in a new marriage.

The *goodness* and *severity* of God (Rom. 11:22) means that although God hates divorce and will stand with a partner for the healing of the marriage no matter what circumstances happen, neither is divorce the unforgivable sin. When people fall short of God's perfect will and truly repent from their hearts, the goodness or grace of God cleanses them of their sins. God's forgiveness carries no penalties. When Jesus talked to the woman at the well who'd had five husbands, He did not tell her she had to stay single the rest of her life.

To anyone reading this chapter who would like to use the grace of God as a "copout" to go ahead and get a divorce instead of working to heal his marriage, let me warn you that if you've read this far, you *know* healing is available, and God holds you responsible for the knowledge you have. To flippantly decide to get a divorce when you know it is against God's will, planning to slide through on the grace of God and repent later, is trifling with God's mercy.

David prayed in Psalm 19:9, 11-13:

The fear of the Lord is clean, enduring for ever: the judgments of the Lord are true and righteous altogether. Moreover by them is thy servant warned: and in keeping of them there is great reward. Who can understand his errors? cleanse thou me from secret faults. Keep back thy servant also from presumptuous sins; let them not have dominion over me: then shall I be upright, and I shall be innocent from the great transgression.

Numbers 15:28-31 tells us the priest would make atonement for the soul that sinned ignorantly. But the soul that sinned presumptuously would bear his iniquity because he had despised the word of the Lord.

Conversely—and this is very important—you cannot get your marriage healed by "legalistically" doing all the things this book instructs. I'm speaking of ritualistically "going through the motions."

Hebrews 11:1 says, "Now faith is the substance of things hoped for, the evidence of things not seen." You must have the substance of faith as evidence of your healed marriage. You may not have it the first time you read this book; you may only get some hope. But don't be discouraged. By meditating on the scriptures, rolling them over and over in your mind and going before God in hours of close communion and prayer, your substance of faith will be developed. You cannot go around in a "milk-toast" attitude, saying, "Well, this book says to bind the devil and quote scriptures, so I am doing all that and this book says that I'll get my partner back."

You not only must do what this book says but also must meditate on the Word and spend much time getting all the scriptures in your heart and mind until you understand what they mean and know God's promises are yours.

It is God's Word that will produce for you. You'll know that you have it because you'll "see" the healing becoming more real to you than the circumstances. When you "know that you know that you know" your marriage is healed *by God's Word* and no one can take it away from you, that's when you have the substance of faith down in your spirit, and it will produce the actual healing.

You begin doing as much as you understand by meditating on and confessing the scriptures, your spirit hears these faith seeds and they become planted in your heart, and soon you have the faith substance necessary for your healing in your mind and spirit. Then your healed marriage is a granted thing in heaven and only a matter of time until it manifests itself on earth.

7

Is There Something An Onlooker Can Do To Affect Healing When Neither Partner Wants It?

Yes, indeed! There is something very important onlookers can do to help heal broken marriages.

Dru and I often have people question how we ever got our terribly broken marriage back together.

"Your marriage was healed because you and Dru were willing to pray together," some say to us.

"Not at the beginning," we respond.

"Your marriage came together because one of you accepted Jesus as your Savior," others say.

"Not at the beginning," we repeat.

The healing of our marriage began because concerned friends prayed.

After Dru and I finally accepted Jesus into our lives and reestablished our marriage on Godly principles, many people came to us and confessed that they had been praying for our marriage for a long time. And we certainly hadn't asked them to.

Only one of these people had spoken directly to us about Jesus, but many others stood in the gap for our salvation with their prayers. Our marriage was not only desperate; it was notorious. For years we wouldn't let most Christians get close enough to us to be of help. But their prayers went where they couldn't go.

Then at the crucial time of the break-up of our marriage, because of this intercessory prayer, God sent Dru to the door of Christian friends; opened her spiritual ears to hear; and they were able to lead her to Jesus and teach her how to use her faith to pray for me.

Often the friends of those who are in a bad marriage become marriage counselors. They listen to one of the partner's stories and say, "I don't blame you. I'd get a divorce too."

The amateur counselor does not realize he is exposing an area in his own life for Satan to attack. In effect, the counselor is admitting that under the same circumstances in his own marriage he too would get a divorce.

Don't forget that divorce is a form of unforgiveness. It is a form of conditional love. It is many things that Jesus isn't, and the Bible instructs us to be like Christ.

Job 22:30 gives this incredibly wonderful promise to concerned intercessors: *"He will even deliver the one [for whom you intercede] who is not innocent; yes, he will be delivered through the cleanness of your hands"* *(Amp.)*.

There is enough comfort and encouragement in this one verse to send us eagerly into prayer and fuel us until the manifestation. This is your *authority*, intercessors, to make the devil back off the ground he has gained and allow God to move in to bring reconciliation to your loved ones just as He did for us.

God responds to His children's prayers. If obedient Christians had not interceded for Dru and me and counseled her according to the Word of God and refused the temptation to pay attention to my declarations that I didn't love her anymore, was getting a divorce, and marrying someone else, our marriage would not have been born again and other marriages would not have been healed through our testimony of the principles we discovered.

My only caution would be that you take it on as a ministry. In other words, a few prayers won't do it. You must determine to intercede for them more perseveringly than the devil has determined to destroy them. This is ministry for true intercessors.

If you feel a calling on your life to be an intercessor and would like some excellent teaching on it, I recommend writing to Dave Roberson Ministries, P.O. Box 54978, Tulsa, OK 74155, for his tapes, "Intercessory Prayer" and "Walking in the Spirit."

I have seen God's time clock for healed marriages diminish dramatically during the last several years. Marriage problems that used to take years to heal are being restored much more rapidly.

People who attend churches teaching sound biblical principles can see their marriages restored more quickly than they ever imagined possible. In the past, many churches taught people how to be born again. Today, they are discovering that God will make *all* things new—including troubled marriages.

Many have been afraid to deal head-on with problem marriages. No one likes confrontation, and a marriage partner who wants out of a marriage is often belligerent toward anyone who suggests otherwise. But those churches accepting God's Word and believing that Jesus' miracle power is capable of correcting *any* problem marriage, are seeing dramatic healings.

Several churches I've spoken at have declared themselves to be "divorce-free." When people come to these pastors for marriage counseling, one of the first things they are told is that divorce is not an option. The only thing the pastors will discuss is healing.

On that basis, marriage partners can't enter counseling sessions "double-minded." They can't come in to criticize their mates and discuss possible biblical escape clauses. The destination—a healed relationship—is established from the start.

We can allow the discouragements of life to chart our futures, or we can change, get on God's program, and walk in healed relationships. We can have the satisfaction of hearing people say, "If you hadn't prayed and believed for us, our marriage wouldn't have worked. If you hadn't walked in unconditional love and given yourself as a sacrifice in prayer, our marriage wouldn't have been healed." Dru and I will be grateful to Lee and Carolyn Huelle throughout eternity.

Recently the Lord spoke to my heart and said, "The world is living like there is no hell." There was a pause, and the thought continued, "And the Christians are living like there is no heaven."

Non-Christians and Christians alike have operated with selfish motives. Both have lived the attitude, "What *I* get out of life now has got to be my principal consideration."

Many, many people travel through life, never making a constructive impact on others. But those who dare to be the influence so clearly needed—who purpose to hold God's standard high for precious families—will have the pleasure of hearing the words, "Well done, thou good and faithful servant."

Helpful Tapes from Born-Again Marriages

The teaching tapes listed below are from Born-Again Marriages seminars and special meetings conducted by Kent and Dru Axtell. The topics are of tremendous benefit to anyone desiring God's best in their own marriage or wanting information for helping others.

Category "A" tapes were taught with a special emphasis on marriage healing. Category "B" tapes deal with strengthening the more mature marriages.

To order simply send in this page or a copy with your check, money order, or MasterCard or Visa # made out to Born-Again Marriages.

Category	Name	Price Each	Quantity	Total Price
A	Healing the Impossible Marriage	$ 4.00		
A	Questions Most Frequently Asked About Marriage Healing	$10.00		
A	Doublemindedness	$10.00		
A	Armor of Light	$10.00		
A	Strife	$10.00		
A	Cause and Effect	$10.00		
B	Marriage Soundness	$ 4.00		
B	Tapping the Power of One Flesh	$24.00		
B	Our Marriage Covenant (pictured on back cover)	$52.50		
A&B	Kent and Dru's Testimony	$ 4.00		

Total Amount Enclosed _____

Card # _____ Exp. Date _____

Signature _____

Name _____

Street _____

City _____ State_____ Zip _____

☐ Please send me information about Standards International.
☐ Please send me information about Nova Shalom.
☐ Please send me information about Repairers and Restorers.
☐ Please send me a complete list of tapes and books.

Send your order to:

Born-Again Marriages ● P.O. Box 8, Council Bluffs, IA 51502

Helpful Tapes from Born-Again Marriages

The teaching tapes listed below are from Born-Again Marriages seminars and special meetings conducted by Kent and Dru Axtell. The topics are of tremendous benefit to anyone desiring God's best in their own marriage or wanting information for helping others.

Category "A" tapes were taught with a special emphasis on marriage healing. Category "B" tapes deal with strengthening the more mature marriages.

To order simply send in this page or a copy with your check, money order, or MasterCard or Visa # made out to Born-Again Marriages.

Category	Name	Price Each	Quantity	Total Price
A	Healing the Impossible Marriage	$ 4.00		
A	Questions Most Frequently Asked About Marriage Healing	$10.00		
A	Doublemindedness	$10.00		
A	Armor of Light	$10.00		
A	Strife	$10.00		
A	Cause and Effect	$10.00		
B	Marriage Soundness	$ 4.00		
B	Tapping the Power of One Flesh	$24.00		
B	Our Marriage Covenant (pictured on back cover)	$52.50		
A&B	Kent and Dru's Testimony	$ 4.00		

Total Amount Enclosed _____

Card # _____ Exp. Date _____

Signature _____

Name _____

Street _____

City _____ State _____ Zip _____

☐ Please send me information about Standards International.
☐ Please send me information about Nova Shalom.
☐ Please send me information about Repairers and Restorers.
☐ Please send me a complete list of tapes and books.

Send your order to:

Born-Again Marriages ● P.O. Box 8, Council Bluffs, IA 51502

Helpful Tapes from Born-Again Marriages

The teaching tapes listed below are from Born-Again Marriages seminars and special meetings conducted by Kent and Dru Axtell. The topics are of tremendous benefit to anyone desiring God's best in their own marriage or wanting information for helping others.

Category "A" tapes were taught with a special emphasis on marriage healing. Category "B" tapes deal with strengthening the more mature marriages.

To order simply send in this page or a copy with your check, money order, or MasterCard or Visa # made out to Born-Again Marriages.

Category	Name	Price Each	Quantity	Total Price
A	Healing the Impossible Marriage	$ 4.00		
A	Questions Most Frequently Asked About Marriage Healing	$10.00		
A	Doublemindedness	$10.00		
A	Armor of Light	$10.00		
A	Strife	$10.00		
A	Cause and Effect	$10.00		
B	Marriage Soundness	$ 4.00		
B	Tapping the Power of One Flesh	$24.00		
B	Our Marriage Covenant (pictured on back cover)	$52.50		
A&B	Kent and Dru's Testimony	$ 4.00		

Total Amount Enclosed _____

Card # _____ Exp. Date _____

Signature _____

Name _____

Street _____

City _____ State_____ Zip _____

☐ Please send me information about Standards International.
☐ Please send me information about Nova Shalom.
☐ Please send me information about Repairers and Restorers.
☐ Please send me a complete list of tapes and books.

Send your order to:

Born-Again Marriages ● P.O. Box 8, Council Bluffs, IA 51502